*Law*Basics

AGENCY

*Law*Basics

AGENCY

By

Aidan ODonnell, BA, LL.B.

Lecturer in Law
Glasgow Caledonian University

EDINBURGH
W. GREEN/Sweet & Maxwell
1998

First published 1998

Published in 1998 by W. Green & Son Limited of
21 Alva Street,
Edinburgh, EH2 4PS

Typeset by Trinity Typesetting,
Edinburgh

Printed in Great Britain by Redwood Books Ltd,
Kennet Way, Trowbridge, Wiltshire

No natural forests were destroyed to make this product; only farmed timber was
used and replanted

A CIP catalogue record of this book is available from the British Library

ISBN 0 414 01230 5

CONTENTS

TABLE OF CASES

SUGGESTED READING

There are currently no Scottish texts devoted solely to the law of agency (although this will be remedied shortly with the publication by the Scottish Universities Law Institute and W. Green of Professor Maher's text). Most of the mainstream books on Scots law include some discussion of the main principles. Some of the more useful include:

Cusine and Forte, *Scottish Cases and Materials in Commercial Law* (2nd ed., Butterworths, 1998).

Gloag, *The Law of Contract* (2nd ed., W. Green, 1929), Chap. 8.

Gloag and Henderson, *Introduction to the Laws of Scotland* (10th ed., W.Green, 1997), Chap. 22.

Gow, *The Mercantile and Industrial Law of Scotland* (1st ed., W. Green, 1964), Chap. 9.

Marshall, *Scots Mercantile Law* (3rd ed., W. Green), Chap. 1.

Marshall, *Scottish Cases on Agency* (1st ed., W. Green, 1980).

Stair Memorial Encyclopaedia of the Laws of Scotland 1932, Vol. 1 1932 pp. 247–280.

Walker, *Principles of Scottish Private Law* (4th ed., Clarendon, 1988).

English Books

Fridman, *Law of Agency* (7th ed., Butterworths, 1996).

Markesinis and Munday, *Outline of the Law of Agency* (3rd ed., Butterworths, 1992).

Reynolds, *Bowstead on Agency* (16th ed., Sweet & Maxwell, 1996).

Stone, *Law of Agency* (Cavendish, 1996).

Articles

Galt, "Mandates" (1989) 39 JLSS 54.

Herd, "The Commercial Agents (Council Directive) Regulations (1993)", 1994 S.L.T. (News) 351.

Hunter, "Boyler v Thomson: Let the Seller Beware", 1996 SLG 3.

Junor, "The Estate Agent's Commission: When is an Introduction Not an Introduction?" (1996) 64 SLG 60.

Leslie, "Negotiorum Gestio in Scots Law", 1983 J.R. 12.

O'Neill, "Compensation, Commercial Agents and Comparative Law", 1997 S.L.T. (News) 141.

Phillips, "Agency: Election and Reflections", 1993 J.R. 133.

Schitt "The Undisclosed Principal: An Anomaly in the Laws of Agency and Contract" (1983) 88 Com LJ 229.

Schmidt, "The Commercial Agents Regulations — Some Unfinished Business", 1996 S.L.T. (News) 13.

Schoire "Commercial Agents: A Fundamental Change" (1994) 15 Business Law Review 171.

Willett, "Buying from a Friend of a Friend" (1995) 225 SCOLAG

1. INTRODUCTION

Agency is a legal relationship which involves three people (a tripartite relationship): an agent, a principal and a third party. The function of the agent is to bring the principal and the third party together in a contractual relationship. The agent is a type of business matchmaker or "middleman". An agent may be an employee of his principal, *e.g.* a sales assistant, or an independent contractor, *e.g.* an estate agent. Not all employees will be agents for their employers, only those whose job it is to bring third parties into a contractual relationship with the employer. Checkout operators in a supermarket will therefore be agents for their employer whereas employees who only fill shelves will not be. The need for agents is obvious. Physical and temporal limitations dictate that a businessman cannot deal with all his customers alone. Even in a small shop the owner will usually need help. The task of his assistant may be perceived purely as selling things to people. However, selling (or buying) involves entering into a contract and thus in law the function of the sales assistant is to effect a contract between the customer (who is the third party) and the employer (who is the principal). The distinctive characteristic of agency is that, although an agent has the authority to effect a binding contract between the principal and the third party, the agent will not generally be a party to that contract and will thus acquire neither rights nor liabilities under it (but see *del credere* agents below at 6).

The main issues in agency are those of authority and trust. These are of concern in the general law of contract, but are more so in agency contracts because of the physical separation that will usually exist not only between the actual contracting parties, but often also between the principal and agent and consequently the increased opportunities that exist for abuse of position. As far as authority is concerned the third party needs to know the extent of the agent's authority (either his actual authority or the authority that will be implied by the courts). Without knowing this he is likely to be wary of dealing with the agent, which would of course frustrate the whole purpose of the agency. A principal needs to trust the agent to carry out the agency with the principal's best interests in mind: the agent needs to trust the principal to indemnify and pay him as agreed. The legal rules relating to these core elements have been developed over many years by the courts, in response to a changing business background.

The law of agency in Scotland had its origins in Roman law, where it was known as the contract of mandate. Roman law, however, never fully recognised agency in its modern form, which involves a two-way relationship between principal and third party with the agent (for the most part) acquiring neither rights nor obligations under the contract he has set up. Mandate was (and still is) different from agency, however, in that it involved a gratuitous obligation between the mandator (principal) and mandatorius (agent). The Roman law of mandate was concerned not with the relationship between mandator and third party, but with the relationship between mandator and mandatorius. What the law of mandate did was to allow one individual to appoint another person to act as his representative.

Bell noted, however, that with the passage of time "instead of the amicable and gratuitous mandate, there has been introduced the onerous contract of agency or factory, imposing duties more imperative entitling the principal to more entire reliance on the performance of his orders, and raising with third parties relations of great extent and importance in trade". Agency had, as it were, ceased to be an amateur game and had become professional. (See below at 23.)

English law on agency developed along different lines but it would be fair to say that present-day Scots law on agency has both Civilian and Anglo-American parents, with a battle, perhaps if not for custody, at least for access, being waged by the lawmakers in Brussels. (See Chapter 7 on the Commercial Agents Regulations 1993.)

The main development of the law of agency, as with the development of all branches of law related to trade and commerce, came with the Industrial Revolution and more particularly with the growth in international trade. The latter did not develop in Scotland in any meaningful or successful way until after the events of 1707. It was obvious that the only way that businessmen's interests could be extended beyond their immediate locality was by the appointment of agents (sometimes known as factors) to represent them. The tobacco trade was a classic example. As trade expanded across the globe it was clear that such agents would be working without direct supervision (or usually none at all). As trade and commerce became increasingly complex and sophisticated, so the rules of agency adapted and developed.

Agency is central to our economic life. Markesinis and Munday illustrate the extent of this centrality:

> "Commerce would literally come to a standstill if businessmen and merchants could not employ the services of factors, brokers, estate agents ... and the like and were expected to do everything themselves. These specialised 'middle-men' whose main purpose is to make contracts on behalf of their principals, are to be found in all advanced societies ... (their) activities are an inevitable feature of a developed economy."

The modern law of agency is still mainly a development of the common law. There is little direct legislation on the subject although some provisions of the Partnership Act 1890 and of company law have a bearing on the role of partners and directors as agents Other statutory regulation of agents includes the Prevention of Corruption Acts of 1906 and 1916, the Estate Agents Act 1979 and the Solicitors (Scotland) Act 1980. Regard must also be had to the provisions of European legislation in the form of the Commercial Agents (Council Directive) Regulations 1993 which came into force on January 1, 1994 (see Chapter 7).

DEFINITION OF AGENCY

According to the *Stair Memorial Encyclopaedia* the word "agent" has no precise legal meaning. It does, however, describe agency as the primary legal relationship existing between an agent and a principal as a result of which the agent is empowered to create secondary legal relationships between the principal and third parties. Bowstead defines agency as "a person having express or implied authority to act on behalf of another person called the principal". It is clear from these definitions that the most important elements in the relationship are those of empowerment and authority. Without these there will generally be no agency and the purported principal will not be under any legal relationship. Agency, however, like other areas of law, is subject to exceptions and we shall examine them later.

How the Relationship Works

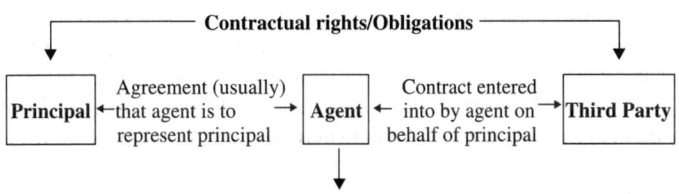

Agency is also an area of Scots law where decisions of the English courts have had a strong influence on the development of the law. This influence has been given judicial recognition and approval. (See Lord Moncrieff in *Rederi Aktiebolaget Nordstjernan v. Salvesen & Co.* (1903)). In this case the pursuers, in the absence of Scottish decisions, sought to rely on a well-settled class of English decisions. Lord Moncrieff said that while these decisions were not, of course, binding on him he had no hesitation in following the law laid down (in England) in so far as it applied to Scotland. He went on to say that in a mercantile question such as the case before him, it was desirable that as far as possible the same rule be applied in both countries. In *Salvesen*, Lord Moncrieff was persuaded to follow English decisions because English law was seen as being "completely settled". In *Copland v. Brogan* (1916), however, the courts chose to adopt the definition of the standard of care required of a gratuitous agent as explained by Bell in preference to that in English cases (where the law on gratuitous agents was then clearly different). *Copland*, however, did not involve "a mercantile question" and, as we shall see later (at 23), it is almost certainly the case that the law regarding gratuitous agents is now the same on both sides of the border.However, there is not always unanimous support for following English precedents (*e.g.* see the difference in opinion between Sheriff McEwan in the *Stair Memorial Encyclopaedia* and Gloag on the liability of undisclosed principals (below at 42)).

DIFFERENT TYPES OF AGENTS

There are many different types of agents and they are appointed in a variety of different circumstances—what follows is only a very brief selection. The label or category attaching to an agent may be useful in attempts to define the agent's authority or obligations. Both Fridman and Stone say that today these labels are not of much practical utility but are useful if only because they can help in understanding some of the authorities, particularly those from the last century. Additionally, the reader will come across them (or be one of them) in his or her professional life, so some background is useful.

The main distinction drawn is between general agents and special agents.

General agents

A general agent is one who has authority to carry out any of the duties which a person of his trade or profession would usually expect to perform. A "managing director" would normally be seen as a general agent of the company and would have authority to enter into a wide range of contracts on its behalf (see *Hely-Hutchinson v. Brayhead Ltd*, below at 33). The same would usually be true of a partner on behalf of his firm.

Special agents

A special agent has a considerably more limited authority. He may only be appointed to carry out a particular transaction, *e.g.* bidding for a specific item at an auction.

Most writers on agency agree that there is little practical use in drawing a distinction between general and special agents. The main value of the distinction is that it is one of the factors which may be used to inform third parties of the nature of the agent's authority and therefore the extent to which he may bind his principal.

The distinction between general and special agents can be seen in *Morrison v. Statter* (1885). Calder was head shepherd on one of Statter's farms. He had occasionally bought and sold sheep for Statter on his special instructions, but both purchases and sales were usually effected by Statter through a salesman. On the occasion in question Calder had been specifically instructed to buy three-year-old sheep at a maximum price of 32s. per head. He bought instead two-year-old sheep at 48s. per head from Morrison. The court held that as Calder had no authority (in the absence of special instructions), Statter was not bound. Lord Young said:

> "Where you have a particular agent employed by a principal, to perform a particular piece of business for him, he must act within the instructions given for the particular occasion, and does not bind his principal if he acts otherwise. If you have a general agent, employed generally in his master's or his principal's affairs, or in a particular department, he is assumed to have all the authority which is necessary to enable him to serve his master as such general agent, or general agent in a particular department."

Solicitors

These are employed by their principals to conduct legal business. Whether or not a solicitor is a general agent or a special agent will depend on the circumstances. The relationship is (as with almost all agents) a fiduciary one and in the event that the agent (solicitor) enters into a contract with the principal (client) it will be closely examined in the event of a dispute. In *Gillespie & Sons v. Gardner* (1909), Lord Dunedin said:

> "it is true that the law looks with some jealousy at transactions between agent and client, but they are not null, merely reducible ... The transaction will not be set aside if the agent can show that he gave full and fair value for what he got ... he did not withhold information ... and did not conceal he was the transacting party."

(For some examples of a solicitor's authority, see below at 33.)

Advocates

Advocates are more likely to be special agents, being employed to carry out a particular or specific piece of business and this will limit their ability to bind their principals. It is presumed that by appearing for a client the advocate has a mandate to do so. The most recent discussion of advocates as agents was in *Brodt v. King* (1991) which revolved around an advocate's right to negotiate on behalf of his client. The court said, quoting Lord President Inglis in *Batchelor v. Pattison & Mackersy* (1876), that the advocate had the right to conduct the case without regard to his client's wishes provided that his mandate had not been recalled and his actions in good faith would bind the client. However, they went on to say that it did not follow that an advocate had authority to enter into an extrajudicial settlement. Lord Fillard said in *Batchelor* that "the principle seems to be that an [advocate] may ... bind his client ... he has no power to make a compromise, involving matters collateral to, or outwith the subject matter of the action". It would seem, therefore, that in the conduct of litigation an advocate has very wide authority to bind his client.

Mercantile agents

The Factors (Scotland) Act 1890, s. 1 defines a mercantile agent:

> "The expression 'Mercantile Agent' shall mean a mercantile agent having in the customary course of his business as such agent, authority either to sell goods or to consign goods for the purpose of sale, or to buy goods, or to raise money on the security of goods."

Mercantile agents may be either factors or brokers.

Factors

The distinguishing characteristic of a factor which distinguishes him from a broker is that he has possession of the principal's goods. He also has the authority to sell them in his own name (*i.e.* as an undisclosed principal (see below at 42)). As a factor has possession of his principal's goods, he can exercise the right of lien against them. An auctioneer is an example of a factor.

Brokers

A broker will differ from a factor in that: (i) he does not have possession of the principal's goods; and (ii) he does not sell in his own name but in his principal's. An example of a broker is a stockbroker or an insurance broker. In spite of the fact that certain agents may usually be labelled as being either a factor or a broker, it is often necessary to look at the precise circumstances of the contract to see if the given categorisation is appropriate in the specific circumstances. *Glendinning v. Hope* (1911) is a good example of the need to do so. In *Cunningham v. Lee* (1874) a solicitor, having bought shares in his own name for a client who failed to pay for them, bought them himself and later sold them. Lord Inglis outlines the distinction between factor and broker:

> "I should be inclined to say that Lee occupied the position of a factor rather than of a broker. Certain distinctions between the offices of broker and factor lead me to this conclusion. Thus a broker buys and sells, not in his own name, but in the name of his principal, whereas a factor buys in his own name. Again, a broker has no possession of the subject, no control over it, no power of disposal. The factor has such powers and a consequent lien over the subjects. In these respects Lee was rather a factor than a broker."

Partners

Under section 5 of the Partnership Act 1890 each of the partners in a partnership is an agent of his fellow partners. The statute says: "Every partner is an agent of the firm and his other partners for the purpose of the business of the partnership". A partnership will therefore be bound to honour transactions carried out in its name by any of the partners, provided of course that these were within the ordinary course of the partnership business. This rule will apply notwithstanding the firm's internal arrangements as to management responsibility, unless the third party knows that the partner lacks the authority to carry out the act in question (Partnership Act 1890, s. 8) (see also below at 35).

Company directors

A company is not a natural person. Somebody therefore has to act on behalf of the company. This is normally done by the directors. Companies will usually delegate considerable authority to the company directors—*e.g.* the Companies (Tables A to F) Regulations 1985 (S.I. 1985 No. 805), Table A, Article 70 provides that: "[T]he business of the company shall be managed by the directors who may exercise all the powers of the company". It should be noted that the authority delegated to company directors is delegated to them collectively. Collectively the directors may sub-delegate this authority, usually to a managing director.

***Del credere* agents**

A *del credere* agent (defined by Bell: *Principles*, s. 286) is usually a mercantile agent who agrees to indemnify the principal if the third party defaults on payment. In return for this the *del credere* agent will be paid a higher rate of commission. Basically, what he is doing is guaranteeing the solvency or creditworthiness of the third party. He is not, however, a party to the contract between principal and third party, and he will normally not be liable to the latter (but see Agent's Liability, below at 33). The form of agency was traditionally most commonly used where goods were being sold abroad, and the principal had concerns regarding whether the third party would pay. Today this concern is normally dealt with by the use of documentary credits or credit guarantees, although the reader may still occasionally come across *del credere* agents (at least in some of the case reports).

Estate agents
Estate agents are employed by clients who wish to sell heritable property. The function of the estate agent is to introduce prospective purchasers to these sellers (or in some cases a seller to a prospective purchaser). Estate agents differ from most other agents in that they will generally not have the authority to effect a binding contract between their principal (usually the seller) and the third party (generally the would-be purchaser). This will normally be done on behalf of the principal by their solicitor. There, is however, a general acceptance that even if estate agents do not fall within the classical definition of an agent, they are still governed by the general rules that apply to agents. Evidence of this can be seen by a quick trawl through the agency section of the *Current Law Monthly Digests*, where estate agents will feature most months, usually in connection with their right (or not) to commission (see Chapter 2). In addition to the common law, estate agents are regulated by the Estate Agents Act 1979 and the Property Misdescriptions Act 1991. It should be noted, however, that the 1979 Act does not define an estate agent but defines "estate agency work". This is because much "estate agency work" is carried out by people who would not normally be described as estate agents. An example is a solicitor. Solicitors are (amongst others) expressly excluded from the provisions of the Act although they are not excluded from the provisions of the 1991 Act.

Not every person whom the law regards as an agent will necessarily so describe himself, *e.g.* a director is an agent for the company, a partner for the partnership and some employees for their employers. To make matters slightly more confusing, many who describe themselves as agents are not agents in the eyes of the law. For example, a car dealer may be described as a BMW agent. However, the car dealer is not usually acting on behalf of BMW when he sells a car but on his own behalf. The contractual relationship is between the customer and the car dealer. There has been, of course, a separate contractual relationship under which BMW supplied the car to the dealer. There is no contractual relationship between the customer and BMW, as there would be if there was an agency in the true legal sense. This is why if there is a problem with the car the customer must look to the dealer for redress, not (at least in contractual terms) to the manufacturer. Some problems may, of course, give rise to an action in delict or tort against the manufacturer.

2. BECOMING AN AGENT

The extent of the authority of the agent is all-important and is discussed in Chapter 4. This chapter examines how the principal–agent relationship is formed. Subsequent chapters will discuss the obligations of the two parties towards each other, their respective relationship with third parties and the ways in which the relationship is terminated.

There are several ways in which a person can become an agent.

EXPRESS APPOINTMENT OF THE AGENT

The express appointment of an agent may be made orally or in writing. The written appointment may be made by granting a power of attorney or a factory and commission, or may be much less formal, *e.g.* a fax. The advantage for both principal and agent of a written appointment is that it will be easier to prove the extent of an agent's authority in the event of a dispute. In the event of a dispute about the existence or extent of an agent's authority parole evidence can be used. In *Pickin v. Hawkes* (1878) a dispute arose as to whether the pursuer was an employee (it being incompetent to prove the existence of a contract of service by parole evidence), the court held that as the contract between the parties had agency as its fundamental characteristic, and in those circumstances parole evidence was competent.

IMPLIED APPOINTMENT OF THE AGENT

The agency relationship may arise by implication. For example, the appointment of a partner will make the partner an agent of the partnership and of the other partners where partnership business is concerned (Partnership Act 1890, s. 5). Other examples of agency implied or imposed by statute include s. 44(1)(a) of the Insolvency Act 1986 (only applies in England and Wales), which provides that where an administrative receiver has been appointed, he is deemed to be the company's agent unless and until the company goes into liquidation. In Scotland, under s. 57(1) a receiver is deemed to be the agent of the company in relation to such property of the company as is attached by the floating charge by virtue of which he was appointed. Also, under s. 56(2) of the Consumer Credit Act 1974, where, *e.g.* a car dealer conducts negotiations with a customer which lead to a credit agreement being entered into between the customer and a finance company, these negotiations will be deemed to be conducted by the car dealer in his capacity as agent (for the finance company) as well as in his actual capacity.

Whether the garage is an agent will, however, depend on the circumstances of the case. In *Powell v. Lloyds Bowmaker Ltd* (1996), a garage had agreed to take a Vauxhall Cavalier in part-exchange for a new Nissan car and to discharge the outstanding hire-purchase payments to Lloyds who had provided the original finance on the Vauxhall. The garage failed to make this payment and Powell brought proceedings against Lloyds on the basis that the garage had been acting as the agent of Lloyds further to the Consumer Credit Act 1974, s. 56, or generally at common law. It was held that the garage was not acting as the agent of Lloyds either under s. 56 or at common law. The garage would be an agent of Lloyds by virtue of s. 56 only in respect of "goods sold or promised to be sold". The agreement was in respect of the trade-in and not the new car and, therefore, s. 56 did not apply.

At common law a director is an agent of the company by implication. A ship's captain is by implication the agent of the owners, as can be seen in *Barnetson v. Petersen Brothers* (1902), where the court held that where the captain accepted the services of a shipbroker, which were to the advantage of the shipowners, they were liable to the broker. Where the agency has been constituted by implication it will terminate either by passage of time and/or a material change of circumstances. In such circumstances there is no need for notice to be given to terminate the relationship. In *Ferguson and Lillie v. Stephen* (1864), the pursuers had for several years supplied clothes to the defender and his sons when they lived in Glasgow. The defender was billed and settled the accounts. After a lapse of several years—during which time the father had been staying in Dundee—the sons, who were by then living independently, ordered a large quantity of clothes to be delivered to them in Edinburgh, where they lived. The court held that Stephen was not liable to pay for the clothes: "the dealings which he had authorised had been long before, were different in kind, and the goods were sent to his own house". This was not so in the present case. Equally, many employees will be agents by implication. Whether or not an employee is an agent will depend on the employee's role.

In *MacKenzie v. Cluny Hill Hydropathic Co. Ltd* (1908), it was held that a hotel manager was an agent by implication. Theatre managers (in *Finburgh v. Moss Empires Ltd* (1908)) and shop managers (see *Tyler v. Logan*, below at 26) have also been held to be their employers' agents but, in contrast, it has been held that a hotel gardener, a stage assistant and a store security guard are not agents by implication. The reason for these decisions seems reasonably obvious, given that the latter trio have no contractual function with third parties. In the recent case of *Lord Advocate v. Chung* (1995), the court was faced with deciding whether or not the relationship of father and son, while they were still alive, *per se* gave rise to an agency. In *Chung* the son had signed an undertaking to the Inland Revenue to pay outstanding tax owed by his deceased father. He had signed the letter "as representative" (of his deceased father). Lord McCluskey said that the relationship of a father and son did not *per se* give rise to an agency relationship, and in any event agency was a relationship that was terminated by death and obviously, therefore, a relationship of principal and agent could not have been created after the death of the putative principal. As there was no principal there was no agent and the son was therefore personally liable, the term "representative" being merely descriptive.

A more recent discussion of the limited scope of agency by implication (or not) can be seen in *Powdrill v. Murrayhead Ltd* (1997) which arose out of the collapse of the Clydesdale Electrical Group in 1994. The defenders had been appointed as advertising agents for the pursuers. They placed adverts in the *Daily Record* for Clydesdale. The *Record* retrospectively paid Murrayhead discounts related to the level of advertising. The discount was used to offset Clydesdale's fees to Murrayhead. When Clydesdale went into liquidation their liquidators claimed sums of retrospective discounts still in the hands of the advertising agency on the grounds that the agency had received the money in its capacity as agent. Murrayfield argued that it entered into the advertising agreements with the paper "as principal and not as agent for the company [Clydesdale]". It was accepted by the court that there was a custom and practice recognised by those involved in the advertising industry that an advertising agent contracts as a principal and not as an agent, unless it is specifically agreed that it should contract as an agent. The significance of this is that the advertising agency is liable for the cost of any adverts it places, and will include this cost in the client's bill. (This was why the advertising agents in the *Hedley Byrne & Co. v. Heller & Partners* (1964) case sought credit references in respect of their clients.) The advertising agent is therefore another example of an "agent" who is not in fact an agent in the strict legal sense.

RATIFICATION OF AGENCY

Becoming an agent by ratification differs from the previous two methods in that the principal may not have authorised the agent to act at all, or may have authorised the agent to act in one particular transaction but the agent has exceeded that authority and contracted in a different transaction. Ratification comes, if at all, when the "principal" decides effectively to condone the lack of authority and retrospectively bind himself to the transaction in question. If, however, he chooses not to do so the agent is left with personal liability under the contract.

There are limits on the appointment of an agent by subsequent ratification. Before there can be an agency by ratification the following criteria must be satisfied.

(a) The agent must have claimed to be acting on behalf of a principal and to have named him. An undisclosed principal cannot ratify: *e.g.* in *Keighley, Maxsted & Co. v. Durant* (1901) an agent, Roberts, had been authorised by Keighley, Maxsted to buy wheat at a certain price. He bought at a higher price. Roberts contracted in his own name but the purchase was intended by him to be a joint one with the plaintiffs. Durant, the seller of the wheat, was not aware of this fact. Keighley, Maxsted later agreed to take it but in the event Roberts and Keighley, Maxsted refused delivery of the wheat. When Durant tried to sue Keighley, Maxsted for damages arising from this breach the House of Lords held he could not do so. Keighley, Maxsted's purported ratification of Roberts' unauthorised act (by first agreeing to take the wheat) was ineffective as Roberts had disclosed neither the name nor the existence of his principal. In a situation like this the only option open to the third party is to raise an action against the purported agent. The result of the decision in *Keighley*, however, is at odds with the generally accepted rule that an undisclosed principal can sue or be sued on a contract even although the third party was unaware of his existence. (See below at 42.)

(b) The principal must have been legally capable of doing the act in question, (1) when the agent made the contract, and (2) at the date of purported ratification. The classic example of this was that a contract, which was entered into by the directors of a company and which was one which the company was not capable of making (it being *ultra vires*, or beyond the company's powers), could not be ratified by the company even if all the shareholders wished to do so. This is no longer the case. A contract which is beyond the powers of a company may now be ratified by a special resolution of the company (Companies Act 1985, s. 35(3)). Another example of the principal lacking contractual capacity (and therefore unable either to do or ratify the act) is seen in *Boston Deep Sea Fishing and Ice Co. Ltd v. Farnham* (1957), where it was held that a French company could not ratify the acts of a purported agent. The acts they wished to ratify had taken place in 1940. As France was under German occupation at the time, the French company was an enemy alien, and therefore lacked contractual capacity.

(c) The principal must have been in existence both at the date of the contract and of the ratification. As is evident from the case of *Kelner v. Baxter* (1866), this can cause problems for company promoters and indeed anyone who purports to contract on behalf of a company before its incorporation. In *Kelner*, the plaintiff sold wine to the defendant, who said he was acting on behalf of a company which was about to be formed. On incorporation, the company sought to ratify the contract made by the defendant. It was held that it could not do so as it (the company) was not in existence at the time the contract was made. In such a case the promoters who make the contract are personally liable (Companies Act 1985, s. 35(4)) (see also *Tinnevelley Sugar Refining Co. Ltd v. Mirrlees, Watson and Yaryan Co. Ltd* (1894). The Tinnevelley Co. was being promoted by Darley and Butler. Before the company was incorporated they contracted for the supply of machinery on behalf of the company. After incorporation when the machinery was delivered, the company found that it was defective. It sued the defenders. The court held that it had no title to sue on a pre-incorporation contract. Darley and Butler could not be "the agents" of a non-existent company. As the company was not in existence when the contract was made, it could not ratify the contract). (See also *Cumming v. Quartzag Ltd*, below at 44.)

(d) The principal must ratify the act in time. There may be a period laid down. In *Goodall v. Bilsland* (1909) the agent (a solicitor) had been employed to object to the granting of a pub licence. His objection failed and the solicitor, without authority from his clients, appealed. His appeal succeeded. The pub owner claimed that the decision of the appeal court should be set aside as the solicitor had no authority to appeal. The clients then attempted to ratify the solicitor's actions. It was held that they could not do so because their attempt fell outwith the 10-day period which was allowed for lodging appeals. *Goodall v. Bilsland* illustrates not only that power of attorney or mandate will be strictly construed by the courts but additionally that it is not enough that the agent acts in time (where there is as here a time-limit)—the principal must also ratify in time for the ratification to be effective. English authority for this can be seen in *Dibbins v. Dibbins* (1896) where two partners, O and P, agreed that on the death of either of them the survivor would have the right to buy the deceased's shares provided he gave notice to the executors within three months. O died. Within three months of the death A, acting on P's behalf but without his authority, informed O's executors that P intended to exercise the option. P did not ratify A's actions until the three months had passed. It was held that the ratification was ineffective. If there is no time-limit the ratification must occur within a reasonable time and what is reasonable will depend on the circumstances. The English courts have reached different decisions as to what fits within "a reasonable time" as far as the ratification of contract is concerned. In *Metropolitan Asylum Boards (Managers) v. Kingham* (1890) it was held that a contract cannot be ratified after the time for its performance or the start of performance. However, Packer J. disagreed with this view in *Bedford Insurance Co. Ltd v. Instituto de Resseguros do Brazil* (1984). His view was that a principal could ratify a contract after the time for its performance provided the ratification benefited the third party. Also, in the case of *Grover and Grover Ltd v. Matthews* (1910), a contract of insurance had been taken out by an agent on his principal's behalf but without his authority. The principal did not ratify the contract until after the insured property had been destroyed by fire. The Court of Appeal held that the ratification was too late and was ineffective as was therefore the insurance policy. The Marine Insurance Act 1906, s. 86 provides that contracts of marine insurance, even those entered into by persons lacking authority, are an exception to this rule provided that the contract was entered into in good faith.

(e) The principal must have had full knowledge of all the relevant facts. Acquiescence and ratification must be founded on a full knowledge of the facts. He would not be bound to a contract where the agent had, for example, misdescribed the quality, description, price, etc., of goods or perhaps the identity of the third party unless he indicates that he is happy to ratify no matter what the circumstances. In *Savery v. King* (1856), X on Y's behalf entered into a mortgage agreement which was in fact fraudulent. Afterwards it was clear from Y's behaviour that he purported to ratify the agreement. Y did not, however, know that the mortgage was invalid. It was held that he could not ratify.

There is no clear authority in Scotland as to whether there can be ratification where the agent ostensibly deals as principal. (See Principal undisclosed below at 42.) English law does not permit ratification in such a situation. Lord McNaughten said (in *Keighley*) that the basis for this rule was that civil obligations cannot be created or founded upon undisclosed intention. He said that this had been recognised in England since the time of Edward IV. Gloag says (at p. 143) that the rule should be followed in Scotland. Sheriff McEwan, however, in the *Stair Memorial Encyclopaedia* founds on the Scottish case of *Lockhart v. Moodie* (1877) where the facts are similar to *Keighley, Maxsted* and says that "there seems to be no good reason why the undisclosed principal should not be liable at least up to the sum he authorised the agent to negotiate". *Lockhart* was not referred to by the judges in *Keighley*.

In *Lockhart* there was a joint adventure between Moodie and Mackenzie. Mackenzie had been authorised to buy yarn at a maximum price per unit. He bought the yarn in his own name without disclosing that he was an agent and at a price one farthing (0.1 new pence) per unit over the amount authorised. Upon his bankruptcy his partner was sued for the price, and was found liable to the extent authorised. Lord Inglis said:

"I do not think that the circumstance that he agreed to give a farthing more than he was authorised ... deprives him of the character of agent. He may not bind his principal to a greater amount than he was authorised to bind him but he will not make himself anything other than an agent."

It should be noted that there is no discussion at all in Gloag as to why the *Keighley, Maxsted* decision should be followed and there would seem to be at least something to say for Lord Inglis's view that the fact that he agreed to pay one farthing more did not affect the existence of the agency. Sheriff McEwan says in the *Stair Encyclopaedia* that there seems to be no good reason why the undisclosed principal should not be liable at least up to the sum he authorised the agent to negotiate. It could also be argued that buying at such a marginally greater sum would in any event be within the implied authority of the agent. There would seem to be a conflict of legal opinion here and all the courts might seek to do would be to seek an equitable solution.

EFFECT OF RATIFICATION

The effect of the principal ratifying a contract (subject to the limitations above) is to make the principal retrospectively liable on the contract from the time it was made. In *Bolton Partners v. Lambert* (1889), the defender offered to buy a factory from the pursuers. The offer was accepted by the pursuers' managing director who did not have the authority to sell the factory. Following a disagreement, Lambert withdrew his offer and several days later Bolton Partners sued him for breach of contract. Eleven days after this the directors ratified the managing director's actions. Lambert argued that the ratification was too late, coming as it did after his withdrawal from the contract. The court held that the ratification acted retrospectively and therefore Lambert was in breach of contract. A deciding factor in the decision was that Lambert was unaware of the lack of authority and hence the need for his actions to be ratified. He must therefore have believed that he had entered a binding contract, withdrawal from which would have left him open to an action for breach.

The above decision has been criticised but Lord Salvesen said of it in *Goodall v. Bilsland* that "there are grounds on which it may be supported" and it has been followed in other more recent cases (*e.g. Presentaciones Musicales SA v. Seconda* (1994)). As we saw above, the ratification must take place within a reasonable time. In *Bolton* it seems that the two-week period between Lambert's withdrawal and the ratification fell within acceptable limits. If the third party was aware of the need for the contract to be ratified he could withdraw at any time before ratification.

AGENCY BY NECESSITY

The concept of agency arising through necessity is strictly speaking an English one but it is a form of the Scots doctrine of *negotiorum gestio* (management of affairs). In *Bannatine's Trustees v. Cunninghame* (1872) the court discussed the responsibility of the *negotiorum gestor*. It said, quoting Erskine (at III, iii, 3):

"By some tests of the Roman law, the *negotiorum gestor* ought to use the most exact diligence ... but in truth the kind of diligence ever rises or falls according to the views of the *gestor* in undertaking the management and the nature of the *gestio*. Where the *gestor* from friendship and necessity takes upon himself the direction of an affair which requires immediate execution ... he is liable only for gross omissions."

The liability of agents of necessity is similar to that ascribed by Erskine to *negotiorum gestors*.

The term "agent of necessity" is, however, in common use in Scotland. Agency by necessity arises where, because of an emergency, one party acts on behalf of another although he has not been asked to do so. Agency of necessity will only arise where the interests of one party are at stake, he cannot be contacted, and some action is taken in good faith on his behalf.

Great Northern Ry v. Swaffield (1874) is both an example of the principles applying to agency of necessity and also of the ridiculous things people will find to fight over. The defendant sent an unaccompanied horse by rail from London to Bedfordshire. Upon arrival, there was nobody to collect the horse. The station staff had no way of contacting the defendant so they had the horse stabled overnight. Swaffield objected to paying the 6d. (2.5p) stabling charge on the ground that he had not authorised it. The dispute dragged on until the stabling bill was £17. The railway company paid this, delivered the horse to Swaffield and claimed that they had acted as agents of necessity and should therefore be reimbursed for their outgoings. The court held that they had acted as agents of necessity because: (1) there was an emergency; (2) they could not contact Swaffield; and (3) they had acted in his best interests.

Whether or not there is an emergency will be a matter of fact. It is not enough that action is taken to avoid inconvenience (*Sachs v. Miklos* (1948)). In *Prager v. Blatspiel* (1924) an agent had purchased skins for his principal but because of the outbreak of war he could neither send the skins to nor contact the principal. He sold the skins on the basis of necessity. It was held that he was not an agent of necessity as the skins could easily have been put in storage. Obviously this would not have been the case had the goods been perishable.

Agency by necessity arose quite frequently in the past, for example where perishable goods were delayed in transit and were sold on the owner's behalf before they became worthless. Improved communications mean that it is much less likely to arise today but it would arise in more mundane circumstances than in *Swaffield*. If your neighbours were climbing in the Himalayas and you had their vandalised window repaired you would be an agent of necessity and could claim that your neighbours reimburse you for the cost of the glazier's bill. When acting as an agent of necessity you would be expected to exercise reasonable care (see *Kolbin & Sons v. Kinnear & Co. (S.S. "Altai")* below at 23). The most recent discussion of agency of necessity is *Eagle Recovery Services v. Parr* (1997), which involved the right of a garage acting on police instructions to be paid for recovering burnt-out vehicles which were a danger to the public. The recovery work was carried out by the plaintiffs. They recovered a burnt-out vehicle from a school playing field. They later claimed the cost of recovery and storage from the owner's insurers. They refused to pay on the ground that there was no contractual nexus between insurer and plaintiff. The court held that an agency of necessity would require: (1) lack of instructions from the owner of the burnt-out vehicle; (2) action needed to protect the public; (3) to be in the best interests of all parties; (4) to be reasonable and prudent; and (5) to protect the owner's interests. As all of these applied, the recovery work had been done as an agency of necessity and the insurers had to pay the garage's reasonable costs. The requirements laid down in *Eagle Recovery* are no more than a refinement of those in *Swaffield*.

CONTRACTUAL CAPACITY

There may be a contract between the agent and the principal and this will generally be the case in the business world. If there is, then both agent and principal must have the necessary contractual capacity. The function of the agent generally is to bring principal and third party together in a contractual relationship to which the agent will not be a party. In this role, therefore, the absence of contractual capacity on the part of the agent may well be irrelevant but, of course, in the business world the agent will need contractual capacity to contract with the principal.

Gow, in *Mercantile and Industrial Law of Scotland* (at p. 16), gives the example of a father sending his pupil son into a shop to buy a bottle of lemonade. There is no contract between father and son. They are in law, however, principal and agent or mandant and mandatory. It is the capacity of the principal that is important, so a principal who lacks contractual capacity cannot increase his capacity by employing an agent of full capacity (see *Boston Deep Sea Fishing and Ice Co. Ltd v. Farnham* at 11).

---

3. THE RELATIONSHIP BETWEEN PRINCIPAL AND AGENT

In most cases the relationship between principal and agent and their specific obligations, one to the other, will depend on the contract between them. Such a contract, as we have seen, may be written or oral, or may arise by implication or necessity. To avoid, or at least lessen, the opportunity for dispute, it is preferable that the contract is embodied in some form of written document no matter how informal. Agent and principal are free to agree whatever terms they wish provided they are not unlawful; the relationship is, after all, a consensual one.

Where commercial agents are concerned, regard should also be had to the Commercial Agents (Council Directive) Regulations 1993 (S.I. 1993 No. 3053). These regulations became operative on January 1, 1994 and implement Council Directive 86/653/EEC. They apply to self-employed commercial agents and their principals, and deal with remuneration and the conclusion and termination of the agency contract. (See also Commercial Agents (Council Directive) (Amendment) Regulations 1993 (S.I. 1993 No. 3173; and see Chapter 7.)

There are, however, terms implied by common law into the relationship. As with all contracts, there are rights and obligations due and owed by each party one to the other.

THE RIGHTS OF THE AGENT

Remuneration
Whether or not the agent is entitled to a fee or commission will depend on the express or implied terms of the contract. Generally speaking mercantile agents, such as auctioneers, stockbrokers, shipbrokers and insurance brokers, are entitled to be paid but this presumption can be rebutted, as in the case of *Dinesmann v. Mair* (1912). In that case it was held that, by custom of trade, the agent had to rely for his remuneration on the proceeds of sale of the herrings which had been consigned to him. In short, if he sold no herrings he would not be entitled to any commission. This type of arrangement is quite common in some sales jobs, usually in situations where the agent (salesman) is self-employed.

The agent's right to remuneration will, of course, arise only when he has carried out the task he was retained to do. Whether or not he has done this may be a matter of dispute. One of the areas where disputes will most frequently arise will be where an agent has been used to effect the sale of a house. The principal (seller) may claim, perhaps with justification, that the resultant sale owed more to his efforts than to the agent's.

In general the courts will examine the circumstances to discover if the result achieved can be attributed to the efforts of the agent and, if it can be, the agent will be entitled to be paid. In *Walker, Fraser & Steele v. Fraser's Trustees* (1910), the pursuers were employed by Fraser to sell his estate. A prospective purchaser, Scott, who had inquired after another property was also sent details of Fraser's estate. He made no move to purchase it, but three years later he specifically requested details, again making no move to purchase. The following year Scott placed a "wanted ad" in the *Glasgow Herald* for an estate. Fraser sent him details, and Scott subsequently bought the estate direct from Fraser. Walker, Fraser and Steele claimed the commission on the sale. Lord Dundas said that whether or not they would be entitled to commission would depend on whether the sale was brought about or materially contributed to by them; did they by their efforts contribute in a substantial degree to the sale? He felt that they had and were therefore entitled to the commission. More recently, in *Chris Hart (Business Sales) Ltd v. Currie* (1992), Currie had retained Hart to sell his pub, with commission being payable "upon completion of a concluded contract for the sale of the premises". An offer to purchase was received and missives of sale and purchase were completed, the missives being conditional on the licence being transferred to the purchaser. The transfer did not materialise and the missives fell. Hart claimed commission of £3,362. The court held that commission was payable. Lord Caplan said "If missives are concluded then the agents have been successful ... and are entitled to their commission". In *Hart* Lord Mayfield said that he did not find reference to English cases to be helpful (as the law relating to property transactions is different). However, much will obviously depend on the particular circumstances of the individual case.

In *Harwood v. Smith* (1997) it was held that an estate agent who had been granted sole selling rights over a property was not entitled to commission where during the agency agreement, but without any involvement by the estate agent, the vendors answered an advertisement from prospective purchasers which led to a sale of the property after the agency agreement had expired. Hobhouse L.J. held that the seller was only liable to pay commission where the sale took place after the termination of the agency if: (a) the agent had introduced the purchaser, or (b) the agent had negotiated with the purchaser on the seller's behalf. This had not been the case and the estate agents were not entitled to commission.

In *Walker, Fraser* Lord Dundas said that an actual introduction of the purchaser to the seller was not a necessary element in a claim for commission; it was enough that he was introduced to the property. This had not happened in *Harwood*. The decisions (or at least the rationale) seem consistent. The agent will be entitled to the agreed commission even although the contract is not completed as arranged, if the non-completion can be laid at the door of either principal or third party. In *Dudley Bros & Co. v. Barnet* (1937) the pursuers had arranged the assignation of a lease held by the defender. Commission had been agreed on the basis of "business resulting from our efforts". The defender, however, assigned the lease to another party. The court held that the pursuers were entitled to be paid the agreed commission. All that was meant by "business resulting" was that the pursuer found a customer who was ready and willing to take on the lease ... and this did not mean in the event of a sale going through to completion. The only reason the sale was not completed was the action of the defender. The agent's right to remuneration will usually end upon termination of the agency. In *Gardner v. Findlay* (1892), the agent had acted for many years as the factor of tenement property. The principal sold the houses. The agent claimed that there was a trade custom which entitled him to commission on rents that would have been due had the property not been sold. The court rejected this argument. In many circumstances there will be provision for commission to be paid after the termination of the agency.

A typical example of this is in insurance, where there will usually be provision for renewal commission to be paid to the agent who originally effected the contract, even although he is no longer agent for the principal. (A recent discussion of these issues can be found in *Marshall v. N.M. Financial Management Ltd* (1997).) There is specific provision in the Commercial Agents Regulations (see Chapter 7 at 60) for "post-termination" remuneration.

The agent's right to remuneration may be lost if he is in breach of contract with the principal. (See *Graham v. United Turkey Red Co. Ltd* (1922), below at 22.)

In the absence of express provision as to remuneration, the customary rate should be paid, *e.g.* fees determined by a professional body. If there is neither an express provision nor an implied one, the agent will be paid on the basis of *quantum meruit* (or what the services rendered deserved). This, as the reader will recall, is a quasi-contractual remedy, an example of which can be seen in *Kennedy v. Glass* (1890) where, in a dispute between Kennedy (an architect) and Glass (a dealer in old machinery) over commission due to the former, the court rejected the architect's claim for £250 commission which he claimed had been agreed but held him entitled to £50 on account of the time spent by him on negotiations.

Relief

The principal must relieve the agent of all losses, liabilities and expenses incurred by the agent in the course of the agency. *Dinesmann v. Mair* (1912) would suggest that the agent is entitled to deduct his expenses from the proceeds of goods he has sold on his principal's behalf. In *Drummond v. Cairns* (1852) Drummond instructed Cairns to buy him shares. Drummond did so and informed Drummond of the fact. When the time came for Drummond to settle the account, Drummond would not pay and Cairns was forced to sell the shares at a loss. Drummond had to reimburse Cairns for the difference between the prices.

The principal need not indemnify an agent who has acted illegally or carelessly and without skill and care. For example, in *Davison v. Fernandes* (1889), the plaintiff was a stockbroker who sold shares for the defendant after having quoted a wrong selling price, which was what induced the defendant to sell. When the defendant discovered the error he repudiated the contract. In accordance with Stock Exchange rules the plaintiff had to compensate the would-be purchaser. He then sought to be relieved of this liability by the defendant, but the court held that his negligence in quoting the wrong price barred him from any right of relief. *Tomlinson v. Liquidators of Scottish Amalgamated Silks Ltd* (1935) is authority for there being no right of relief where an agent has incurred expenses in defending himself against criminal charges. Tomlinson was a promoter and director of Scottish Amalgamated Silks Ltd. The company went into voluntary liquidation. Tomlinson was charged and tried for fraud on the basis that he had issued a fraudulent prospectus and had misapplied company funds. In the event, he was acquitted and sought to recover from the liquidator the expenses incurred in his defence which amounted to some £11,500. He based his right of relief both on common law and more specifically on the articles of association of the company, which provided for the indemnification of any director against all costs, losses and expenses which he might incur by reason of any act done by him as a director. It was held that he was not entitled to be relieved of this liability either at common law or under the articles as the expenses were incurred in a "mere personal misfortune which overtook him" and not as part of his duties as a director. Although on the face of it this may seem harsh, it is clear from the report of the case that the allegations which resulted in Tomlinson being charged would never have been actions properly incurred in the course of his agency.

Lien

The agent has a right of lien over any of the principal's property which is in his possession as a result of the agency. A lien is the right of a creditor to retain moveable property belonging to the debtor but entrusted to the creditor's possession for some purpose, until the creditor's claims against the debtor are satisfied. The agent can exercise this right until the principal has paid the agreed remuneration and expenses and relieved him of any liabilities arising out of the contract. Lord Kinnear said in *Glendinning v. Hope* (1911):

> "every agent who is required to undertake liabilities or make payments for his principal, and who in the course of his employment comes into possession of property belonging to his principal over which he has power of control and disposal, is entitled, in the first place, to be indemnified for the monies he has expended, or the loss he has incurred, and, in the second place, to retain such properties as come into his hands in his character of agent."

The right of lien does not allow the agent to sell the principal's goods and it is lost if the agent parts with possession of the goods. Some agents have a general lien, that is the right to retain the principal's property until any sums due by the principal have been paid—the goods retained need not be specifically related to the payments due. It is recognised that solicitors, bankers and factors (this would include stockbrokers and auctioneers) have a general lien (see *Glendinning v. Hope,* above) but this right does not extend to a general commission agent. In *Murray v. Bernard* (1869) the pursuer had acted for several years as the sole agent for the defenders who were brewers. They had supplied him with ledgers and other books, on the understanding that the books were to remain Bernard's property. On the termination of the agency Bernard sought the return of the books. Murray wished to keep them until all obligations between them had been finalised. The court held that as Bernard had the greatest interest in the books they were entitled to recover them.

Lord Trayner said in *Drummond v. Muirhead & Guthrie Smith* (1900) that "a law agent in whose hands are the title deeds of the property of his client has undoubted right to retain those deeds in his hands so long as he has a claim against his client". In *Yau v. Ogilvie & Co.* (1985), Yau wished to sue his solicitors for professional negligence. To enable him to do so he needed to recover the file kept by the solicitors relating to his business. He petitioned the court under the Administration of Justice (Scotland) Act 1972. The solicitors argued that they had a right of lien until their fees were paid. Lord McDonald said that "the [solicitors] are entitled ... to withhold production of the file until their business account is paid". The decision of *Findlay (Liquidator of Scottish Workmen's Assurance Co. Ltd) v. Waddell* (1910) would suggest that an auditor or accountant has no comparable general lien to that of a solicitor. Auditors and accountants may, however, have a special lien. As Lord Johnston said in *Findlay*: "he [the auditor] has a right of retention of papers put into his hands for the purpose of the work on which he is employed until he is paid [for] his employment."

The attitude of the courts is that they do not favour the extension of general liens beyond the established categories. A special lien is the right to retain property until any sums owing on that particular piece of property have been paid, *e.g.* a garage could keep your car until you have paid for repairs to it. It would, however, have no right of lien against luggage in the car. In *Meikle and Wilson v. Pollard* (1890) the pursuers were employed by a baker to collect money owed to him. To enable them to do this they had the baker's account books in their possession. When the baker became bankrupt the trustee in sequestration sought delivery of the books. It was held that as the pursuers had not been paid they could retain them until they had been paid.

---

4. THE DUTIES OF THE AGENT

If there is a contract between principal and agent it will usually set out the agent's duties and it is the prime obligation of the agent to carry out these duties. If, however, there is no contract, or if it is silent, there are core agent's duties which are implied by law. These duties will apply unless the contract makes express provision for their exclusion. The relationship of principal and agent is one which involves a special degree of trust. It is what is known as a fiduciary relationship. The case of *Sao Paulo Alpargatas S.A. v. Standard Chartered Bank Ltd* (1985) contains a good discussion of the nature and the extent of an agent's fiduciary duty. The principal entrusts his affairs to the agent; the principal must therefore be able to rely on the agent. This sense of trust could be said to lie at the heart of the principal–agent relationship. Normally, however, the agent must put his principal's interests before his own. It was conceded in *Lothian v. Jenolite Ltd* (1969) that there was no reported case in which it was decided that there was in every contract of agency an implied term that the agent would not compete with his principal. Lord Milligan said that the submission that it was a universal principle that an agent had a fiduciary duty, and that he could not enter into any contract in his own interests if, in doing so, he would be acting against the interests of his principal, unless his principal agreed, was one which imposed a very severe limitation on commercial agency and was not readily implied. This would suggest that the fiduciary duty in a commercial agency would not be at such a high level as it would be in, *e.g.* a trust. Nor was it, he said, of universal application. However, it would be good advice that an agent who fails to put his principal's interests first may be held liable for any consequent loss suffered by his principal.

It may be that the contract between them will expressly prohibit the agent from acting as an agent for other principals, but if that is not expressly mentioned then it will not be implied. Lord Milligan said that while there would normally be no objection to such a prohibition being expressly included it was a very different matter to imply such a term into a written contract. Lord Walker said in *Lothian* that if a principal wished to impose a restriction on an agent then there should be provision for this in the contract. It would, therefore, be permissible for an insurance broker to sell the policies of several different companies unless expressly prohibited from doing so. This, of course, is the position of independent financial advisers who are not tied to the products of a single company. Indeed, in *Kelly v. Cooper* (1992), which involved the rights and duties arising where an estate agent sold two neighbouring houses, the court held that a term was to be implied that in the ordinary course of business an agent was entitled to act for other principals, and to keep confidential from each principal information obtained from other principals. This will surely be true only as long as there is no breach of the duty of good faith (see below at 26). The following duties will be implied in the absence of any express provision to the contrary.

Duty to obey instructions
The agent must carry out his principal's instructions provided that they are lawful and reasonable. An agent who acts contrary to his principal's instructions will usually be personally liable (see *Barkley & Sons v. Simpson* (1897), below). The exact form of these instructions will depend on the nature of the relationship between the parties. For example, someone who wishes to buy or sell a house and uses the services of a solicitor to do so will only give very general instructions often amounting to no more than "sell my house". In such a case, the solicitor must act according to the general established customs of the profession. In the absence of express instructions, the agents must exercise their best judgement provided that they act with the standard of care that would be expected of a competent member of their trade or profession. Lord McLaren said in *Fearn v. Gordon & Craig* (1893):

> "A law agent is not an artificer to carry out mechanically the instructions of his client. He is a legal adviser as well as an executant. The client, in general, is no more capable of telling his lawyer how to proceed in the business for which he is employed, than a patient is able to tell his physician or surgeon how to operate. Accordingly, when a purchaser employs a conveyancer, he is not expected to tell the solicitor what deeds he is to prepare and what enquiries regarding previous transactions are necessary. It is for the solicitor to tell him what is necessary."

In *Turpin v. Bilton* (1843), Bilton, an insurance broker, agreed to effect an insurance policy on Turpin's ship. He failed to do so and when the ship sank uninsured it was held that Bilton was liable in damages to Turpin for the loss. In *Gilmour v. Clark* (1853), Gilmour instructed Clark to take a consignment of goods from Edinburgh to Leith Docks and put them on board *The Earl of Zetland*. The goods were, however, put aboard another vessel, *The Magnet*. *The Magnet* sank. It was held that Clark was liable to Gilmour for the value of his lost cargo. Even where the agent is liable to his principal the latter is under an obligation to minimise his losses. In *Barkley & Sons v. Simpson* (1897), the pursuer principal had instructed his agent to arrange for a coal delivery to be made on to lighters and then on to the gas works who were the end users. The agent failed to do this and the ship carrying the coal delivered it, as was usual, to the quay. The principal refused delivery and the coal was subsequently sold at a loss. Lord Young described the action as "ridiculous" and "extravagant" and refused the pursuer's claim saying that the "only proper course was to have taken delivery of the coal on the quay and charged the agent the extra for the extra expense of carting the coal to the gas works". In *Barkley* the court discussed the liability of an agent who allowed an unauthorised term to remain in the contract, although in this instance he was not held liable, as the principal had not minimised his loss. Adding unauthorised terms to the contract may also incur personal liability on behalf of the agent. In *Bank of Scotland v. Dominion Bank (Toronto)* (1891) the defenders sought payment of money owed to them using the services of the pursuers, who were their Scottish agents. The debtors offered to pay on condition that they paid no interest or expenses. An employee of the pursuers accepted these terms without them being agreed by the defenders for this loss. For reasons that need not concern us but connected to the unauthorised terms the defenders were not paid. The House of Lords held that the Bank of Scotland was liable. Where the agent fails to follow his principal's instructions contained in the contract he will forfeit his right to remuneration during that time. In *Graham v. United Turkey Red Co. Ltd* (1922), Graham, who acted as agent for the defenders, had entered into a restrictive covenant whereby he agreed to sell only the defenders' products. He breached the agreement and when he sought payment for the period of the agency the court held that he was not entitled to payment for the period when he sold other parties' products. Lord Ormidale said that the right to payment depended on performance of the services laid down in the contract. By failing to act as agreed they lost the right to payment.

Duty to exercise reasonable care
All agents are under a duty to exercise reasonable skill and care. Bell (*Principles*, s. 221) said they must act with "the care and diligence of a man of common prudence". Where the agent is a member of a particular trade or profession, he must exercise the appropriate standard of skill and care (*Beattie v. Furness Houlder Insurance (Northern) Ltd* (1976)). More skill is expected of a professional person acting in his professional capacity than is expected of a lay man acting for a friend. The agent's failure to exercise reasonable skill and care may leave the agent open to a claim in damages from the principal. In *Rederi Aktiebolaget Nordstjernan v. Salveson* (see above at 3) the agents (shipbrokers) were employed to obtain a cargo for their principal's vessel. Both third party and principal were mutually unaware of the other's identity. During the course of negotiations it was obvious that there was no agreement on some of the terms of the contract. The agents told both principal and third party that the contract had been concluded on their "terms". These terms were completely different and the "agreement" collapsed. Lord Davey said that by giving the principals incorrect information they were "liable in damages for such a breach of duty". Other

examples of failure to exercise reasonable care include *Alexander Turnbull & Co. Ltd v. Cruikshank and Fairweather* (1905) where the defenders acted as patent agents for the pursuers. One of their duties was to notify the principal when patents had to be renewed. This they failed to do on two occasions and were held liable in damages for the subsequent loss incurred. The *ratio* in *Turnbull* relied heavily on *Stiven v. Watson* (1874) where the agent was not a professional but someone acting as a friend (see below at gratuitous agents). In *Kolbin & Sons v. Kinnear & Co. (S.S. "Altai")* (1931) (see 14) the House of Lords held that the wrongful disposal of goods by an agent who fails to take proper care to safeguard his principal's interests will involve a breach of the duty to exercise reasonable care and leave him liable in an action for damages. This applies even in a case like *Kolbin* where the defenders were agents of necessity. The duty of care owed by agents of necessity is to take reasonable care in the circumstances. In *Kolbin* the defenders had handed over their principal's goods to a third party who sold them but subsequently went bankrupt before accounting for the value of the goods.

Gratuitous agents

Mandate is the name given to a gratuitous contract whereby one person (the mandant) authorises another (the mandatory) to act on his behalf. It is the gratuitous element that differentiates agency from mandate. Given its gratuitous nature, it features little in the business world, but examples can be seen in the context of powers of attorney and proxies to vote at meetings (Companies Act 1985, s. 372).

It does not matter that the agent acts gratuitously; he is still obliged to exercise reasonable care. Roman law imposed a very high duty of care on mandatories but this has not been adopted by Scots law. Erskine said that a gratuitous agent is only liable for such diligence as he employs in his own affairs and this was further expressed by Bell as the duty of "reasonable care". The mandatory's duty to exercise reasonable skill and care can be seen in *Copland v. Brogan* (1916). Brogan, a carriage hirer, had acted as a messenger for Copland, a schoolteacher, on several occasions. He acted gratuitously. On the occasion in question Copland had asked Brogan to cash some cheques for him. Brogan did this but on the way home he lost the money. There was no imputation of dishonesty on Brogan's part. It was held that Brogan had to make good the loss to Copland. The mere fact of the loss without any satisfactory explanation was evidence that Brogan had failed to exercise reasonable care. Reasonable care was defined as being "such care as a man of common prudence generally exercises about his own property of like description" (Lord Justice-Clerk Scott Dickson, quoting from Bell's *Principles* in *Copland v. Brogan*). He declined to follow English authorities as he had difficulty in accepting them as being in conformity with the laws of Scotland. The English authorities seemed to suggest that a gratuitous agent (mandatory) was liable only if gross negligence could be shown. This, of course, would usually be difficult and almost certainly could not have been shown in *Copland* where all that was required was to show that the mandatory had failed to take reasonable care (as defined above). This duty was discussed in the recent English case of *Chaudry v. Prabhakar and Another* (1988), where C had asked P to buy a car on her behalf. He was not a mechanic but had bought and sold several cars in the past. He was not to be paid. C stipulated that she did not want a car that had been involved in an accident. P bought a one-year-old car, the bonnet of which had been crumpled and repaired, but he made no inquiries of the seller as to the car's history. The car was subsequently discovered to be unroadworthy and to have been previously written off. C sued both P and the seller (who had already admitted liability under the Sale of Goods Act 1979, s. 14(2) and had abandoned his appeal). Stuart-Smith L.J. said (quoting Ormerod L.J. in *Houghland v. R.R. Low (Luxury Coaches) Ltd* (1962)).

"'I have always found some difficulty in understanding just what was "gross negligence" because it appears to me that the standard of care required ... is the standard demanded by the circumstances of that particular case ... The question we have to consider in a case of this kind (if it is necessary to consider negligence) is whether in the circumstances of this particular case a sufficient standard of care has been observed ....'"

Stuart-Smith L.J. went on to say that whatever standard of care was required of an unpaid agent, the defendant, in buying a car that was so obviously suspect, had fallen below it. The court held, with some doubts expressed by May L.J. (who felt that the imposition of a *"Donoghue v. Stevenson"* duty of care was not an attractive one), that a gratuitous agent owes his principal a duty of care to exercise the degree of care and skill which could reasonably be expected of him in all the circumstances, that degree of care and skill being measured objectively and not subjectively. The defendant was held to be liable in damages to the plaintiff. It is suggested that the approaches of Lord Justice-Clerk Scott Dickson and Stuart-Smith L.J. are complementary and in no way contradictory.

The Supply of Goods and Services Act 1982, s. 13, affirms the common-law position of both Scotland and England by making the exercise of reasonable skill and care an implied term of all contracts of agency. The section does not, however, apply to Scotland.

Duty to act in person
The relationship of agent and principal is one which involves a high level of trust and therefore the agent is under a duty to act personally. He must, prima facie, carry out his tasks by himself. He must not delegate the performance of his duties to someone else. This is expressed by the maxim *delegatus non potest delegate* (a delegate cannot delegate). This maxim does not, of course, mean that the agent is prohibited from employing clerical and other assistants, and has in any case "almost been eaten up with exceptions" (Gow, *Mercantile Law of Scotland*, p. 530). Much will depend on whether the agent has been chosen for his own particular and unique personal qualities. In *De Bussche* (below) it was said "in as much as confidence in the particular person is at the root of the Agency ... such authority [to delegate] cannot be implied as an ordinary incident in the contract". If this element of *delectus personae* (choice of person) is present then there will be a presumption against delegation. The contract between principal and agent may expressly provide for delegation or it may be implied by custom

of trade or profession. Thesiger L.J. said in *De Bussche v. Alt* (1878): "the exigencies of business do from time to time render necessary the carrying out of the instructions of the principal by a person other than the agent originally instructed for the purpose ...". If delegation is permitted, then there will be a contractual relationship between principal and sub-agent similar to that between principal and agent. However, if the sub-agent fails to carry out his duties, then *MacKersey v. Ramsay Bonar and Co.* (1843) is authority for any liability to the principal falling on the original agent. In *Mackersey* Lord Campbell said that the agent's liability for a sub-agent is not confined to cases where the principal has reason to suppose that the agent will act in person but extends to cases where he knows there will be delegation. An architect has been held to be impliedly authorised to delegate some of his duties to a surveyor (*Black v. Cornelius* (1879)). The danger of relying on implied authority can, however, be seen in a similar case some years later: *Knox and Robb v. Scottish Garden Suburbs Co. Ltd* (1913). In that case, it was held that the architect agent had no implied authority to delegate. The reason for the difference in decisions in the two cases would seem to depend on the stage the contract has reached at the time of the sub-delegation. Lord President Dunedin said in *Knox & Robb* that he had no doubt that when an architect is employed and plans have been agreed and he gets the go-ahead to carry on with the building then, at that stage, he has the right to use the services of such person as a surveyor, without express authorisation from the principal. In *Knox* things were at a much earlier stage and the architect did not have "a free hand" to delegate. Whether or not a solicitor has authority to delegate, *e.g.* to an advocate, will depend on whether the principal knows that the litigation involves an advocate's services. A solicitor has no implied right to instruct an advocate if a case goes to appeal even where the solicitor himself has no right of audience. However, in *Robertson v. Foulds* (1860), it was held that a country solicitor had authority to delegate the handling of Court of Session business to Edinburgh agents.

Duty to keep accounts

The agent is under a duty to keep his property and that of the principal separate, *e.g.* he must not pay money received as agent into his own bank account. In addition to the common law rules on keeping accounts, there may be additional statutory provision, such as the Solicitors Accounts (Scotland) Rules. It is, of course, in the interests of the agent as well as the principal that clear and concise accounts are kept. There is, however, no absolute requirement that these accounts are detailed or are in any standard form recognised by accountants. It may well be that the principal is happy that the agent renders verbal accounts, as in *Russel v. Cleland* (1885) where the younger brother acted as agent for his older brother who was too ill to manage his farm. The younger brother handled all the farm's financial affairs. No accounts were kept as the two met every day. When the older brother died, his trustees sued the younger for an accounting. The court held that as the older brother had been happy with the lack of accounts there was no need for a formal accounting. The accounts must reflect any discounts received. The principal, and not the agent, is entitled to any interest gained from the deposit of money due to the principal. Where a solicitor lodged clients' money in a deposit account in the name of the firm, the firm returned the capital to the clients but kept the interest, which was regarded by the solicitor as his money. In spite of the fact that this practice was acceptable to the Law Society, the House of Lords held that it could not be justified (*Brown v. IRC* (1964)). In the event of any deficiency which cannot be explained, the agent is bound to make good the loss to the principal. In *Tyler v. Logan* (1904), T owned a number of shoe shops and L was the manager of the Dundee branch. There was a discrepancy of some £62 which L could not explain. The court held that even although there was no suggestion of dishonesty (although the sheriff had earlier felt he was civilly liable for negligence), L had to make good the money to T. The appropriate action when there is a liability to account is one of accounting and not damages (see *Brown*). In *Sao Paulo Alpargatas S.A. v. Standard Chartered Bank Ltd* (1985) the pursuer raised an action of damages for breach of fiduciary duty. Lord Grieve felt that an action of accountability would have been more appropriate.

The most recent consideration of the duty to account can be seen in *Yasuda Fire and Marine Insurance Co. of Europe v. Orion Marine Insurance, Underwriting Agency Ltd* (1995) where Colman J. explained that:

> "[the] obligation to provide an accurate account in the fullest sense arises by reason of the fact that the agent has been entrusted with the authority to bind the principal to transactions with third parties and the principal is entitled to know what his contractual rights and duties are in relation to those third parties as well as what he is entitled to receive by way of payment from the agent".

There is, of course, no absolute need for the parties to "account" in the "fullest sense" as outlined by Colman J. (see above, *Russel v. Cleland*).

Duty to act in good faith

The relationship is a fiduciary one (but see above at 20) and therefore whatever the agent does must be done in good faith for the benefit of his principal. He must not allow his personal interests and those of his principal to conflict.

If there is, or is likely to be, any such conflict of interests, the agent must make the circumstances known to the principal. It will then be up to the principal to give or refuse his consent. What amounts to a conflict of interest will depend on the express or implied term of the contract, for as we have seen above it is possible to be an agent for more than one principal.

In *Lothian v. Jenolite Ltd* (1969), it was held that, where the contract of agency is in writing, there is no implied condition that the agent will never, without the principal's consent, act so as to bring his and his principal's interests into conflict. Lord Milligan said:

> "The proposition which the defenders invite us to affirm is that in all agency cases there is an implied condition that the agent will not without the permission of his principal act, even in an outside matter, in such a way as to bring his interests into conflict with those of his

principal. There is admittedly no case in which such a proposition has been affirmed ... If the defenders had wanted to restrict the activities of the pursuer, they could have asked him to agree to their proposed restriction ... they cannot now seek to rectify the position by attempting to discover an implied condition."

It is clear from *Lothian* that the agent's duty to act in good faith is limited to what he does in the course of his agency. Outwith that he is entitled (as a principal is) to put his own interests first.

In *Kelly v. Cooper*, an estate agent, Cooper, was instructed by Kelly to sell a house. The owner of an adjacent house also instructed Cooper to sell his house. This adjacent house was sold first. The purchaser (the American Presidential candidate Ross Perot) then offered to buy Kelly's house (through Cooper). Cooper made no mention to Kelly that he had handled the sale of the adjacent house. Both sales were completed. Kelly claimed that Cooper had breached his duty by failing to disclose information and that there had been a conflict of interest. The court disagreed. The reasoning of the Privy Council was similar to that of Lord Milligan in *Lothian v. Jenolite*. The decision in *Kelly* is also judicial approval that the circumstances of estate agency contracts give rise to an implied contract term that the normal duty of disclosure to principals is displaced. It could not, of course, be otherwise. Had Cooper informed Kelly of his relationship with the owner of the second house he would be in breach of his duty of good faith to the latter. If the agent is a "commercial agent" within the definition in the Commercial Agents Regulations 1993, there is a general non-derogable duty to act in good faith towards the principal imposed on him by regulation 3(1) (see Chapter 7). Estate agents do not, however, fall within the definition of a commercial agent.

There are several aspects of the duty to act in good faith:

(a) the duty not to make a secret profit;
(b) the duty not to misuse confidential information; and
(c) the agent's duty when buying and selling property.

These are dealt with in turn below.

Duty not to make a secret profit

The agent must not use his position to make a profit for himself over and above the remuneration paid to him by the principal. Not all profits earned over and above the remuneration from the principal will be a secret profit. Many agents will by custom receive money over and above what they receive from their principal. A waiter in receipt of tips might be the most obvious example; he is entitled to keep them unless there is some express arrangement or custom that dictates otherwise. The agent will, in many circumstances, find himself faced with the choice of potential third parties all anxious to contract with the principal. In order "to catch his eye" he may be offered some form of inducement and, if he accepts it, he must credit the principal with the amount.

In *Ronaldson v. Drummond & Reid* (1881) a solicitor, who was acting on behalf of trustees, engaged an auctioneer to arrange the sale of some furniture. The auctioneer paid some of his commission to the solicitor. Lord Craighill described this practice as "a most reprehensible one" and hoped it would be the last he heard of it. It was held that the solicitor had to account for the payment to the trustees. It was argued in this case that this custom of split commissions was a custom of trade which presumed the principal's implied consent. The court said that even if this was so it was no defence. In *Ronaldson* the existence of the trade custom was not disclosed to the trustees. This made it much more difficult for it to be seen as fair. In *Turnbull v. Gorden* (1869) the agent had obtained goods on behalf of the principal. He had managed to negotiate a discount on the price. However, he sought to recover the full price from the principal. It was held that he was not permitted to do so. The full benefit had to be passed on to the principal. A similar issue arose in *Solicitors' Estate Agency (Glasgow) Ltd v. MacIver* (1992) where the agency received a discount for block advertisements if placed on behalf of clients. It was held that it had to account to the clients for the value of the discount. The duty to account for all profits extends to what has been described as a "windfall". In *Trans Barwil Agencies (U.K.) Ltd v. John S. Braid & Co. Ltd* (1988), due to an error in converting foreign currency to sterling the agents found themselves with surplus funds. The agents had in fact told the principal that the wrong exchange rate was being used but the principal ignored the advice. The principal then sought to recover this surplus on the ground that it was a secret profit. The court held that they were entitled to do so. Lord McCluskey said:

> "It does not matter if the secret profit results from dishonesty, negligence or mistake; it must be accounted for ... All the agent is entitled to, is the known agreed remuneration. If there should be a windfall, however arising, the agent must account to the principal for it because the principal is entitled to the benefit of it."

Secret profits, or secret commissions as they are sometimes known, also include what are known more colloquially as bribes. The discount in *Turnbull* was held not to be a bribe. A bribe is a payment made to an agent by a third party who knows that the agent is acting on his principal's behalf with the aim of inducing the agent to contract with the third party. The payment is kept secret from the principal. There is a very thin dividing line between a secret profit and a bribe. To quote Lord Denning on another matter altogether, "you will recognise one [a bribe] when you see one". A bribe was defined in *Industries and General Mortgage Co. Ltd v. Lewis* (1949) as the payment of a secret commission under the following circumstances:

(1) a payment is made to the agent;

(2) the third party who makes the payment is aware that the agent is acting as an agent;

(3) the third party fails to disclose to the principal that he has made the payment to the agent.

The definition would seem to suggest that all secret commissions will give rise to a presumption of corruption. However, in *Anangel Atlas Compania Naviera SA v. Ishikawajima-Harima Heavy Industries Co. Ltd* (1990) it was said that the key element in deciding whether a secret commission amounted to a bribe (in addition to the factors above) was "whether or not the making of it gives rise to a conflict of interest, that is to say, puts the agent into a position where his duty and his interest conflict".

If it can be proved that a secret commission was paid or received corruptly then both donor and recipient will be guilty of a criminal offence under the Prevention of Corruption Acts 1906 and 1916. Obviously an agent who is in receipt of a bribe (or secret commission) is unlikely to put the principal's interests first.

In addition to criminal consequences there are consequences under civil law. The principal may dismiss the agent, recover commission paid and refuse to pay any commission due. Payment of secret commissions is a civil wrong, so the third party may be liable in damages to the principal, who may refuse to perform the contract. *In Makesan v. Malaysia Government Officers Co-operative Housing Society Ltd* (1979) the agent, who was a director of the housing association, had entered into a corrupt agreement with a third party over the purchase and resale of land to the society. The agent was paid a bribe of 25 per cent ($122,000) of the third party's profit. The Privy Council held that the principal could recover either the amount of the bribe or the amount of the profit made by the third party (in England the former is a restitutionary remedy while the latter involves the tort of deceit). Earlier authorities had suggested that the principal could recover both the bribe and the third party's profit. The principal will now have to decide between the two, and his decision will almost certainly be based on matters such as the respective sums involved and the physical availability of agent and third party (in *Makesan*, the third party had fled the jurisdiction).

The agent is, of course, entitled to commission earned during the period when there was no breach of faith (see *Graham v. United Turkey Red Co.* (1922) (above at 18)). In *Kelly v. Cooper* (above) the court held *obiter* that an agent who committed an innocent breach of fiduciary duty could recover any commission otherwise payable. The principal need not show that any loss has been suffered as a result of the agent receiving a secret commission. It is enough to show that the agent has made a profit over and above the agreed remuneration.

Duty not to misuse confidential information
In the course of an agency an agent may come into possession of a wide range of information which is commercially sensitive and confidential. Agents must not use this information for any purpose other than that of their principal. This duty may last beyond the termination of the agency. For example, in *Liverpool Victoria Legal Friendly Society v. Houston* (1900), Houston had been an agent of the society but had been dismissed by them. He then gave a list of the society's members, which had come into his hands while an agent, to a competitor, who used it to canvass for business. The court held that the lists were confidential and Houston was not entitled

to use them and could be interdicted from so doing. Lord Pearson said "the law implies a contract that the information shall not then or afterwards be ultroneously disclosed to a third party". The leading English case on misuse of information is *Boardman v. Phipps* (1967) where the agent was a solicitor for a trust. The trust owned shares in a private company. The agent made use of information gained through his agency to buy shares in the private company on his own account. His intention was to protect the interests of the trust and some but not all of the trustees were aware of the transaction. The trust suffered no loss on the purchase (and may indeed have benefited). The agent was still obliged to account for the profit he had made. Lord Denning said of an agent's duty not to misuse information:

> "[L]ikewise, with information or knowledge which he has been employed by his principal to collect or discover, or which he has otherwise acquired, for the use of his principal, then … if he turns it to his own use, so as to make a profit by means of it for himself, he is accountable."

Commercial agents within the meaning of the Commercial Agents Regulations 1993 are, under regulation 3(2)(b), specifically obliged to communicate to their principals all the necessary information available to them (see Chapter 7).

Duty when buying and selling principal's property

It will often be the function of the agent to buy and/or sell property, either heritable or moveable, for the principal. Agents may not sell their own goods to their principal without the principal's consent. The law in this area was succinctly stated by Lord Ardmillan in *Cunningham v. Lee* (1874) where he said that it was "well settled in England and Scotland that an agent cannot purchase what he is employed to sell or sell what he is employed to purchase".

In *Armstrong v. Jackson* (1917), A employed J, who was a stockbroker, to buy shares for him. J already owned some of these shares and he sold them to A without telling A the true position. When A discovered this, he sought to rescind the contract. It was held that he could do so. There was a conflict of interest. As a buyer the agent's aim is to buy goods at the lowest price while as a seller his aim is to get the highest possible price. It was immaterial that the shares were sold at the market price. The principal should have been told. This element of full disclosure is also implied where the agent seeks to buy property from his principal. In *McPherson's Trustees v. Watt* (1877), W was an advocate in Aberdeen who acted as a broker in the sale and purchase of estates. He acted as law-agent (solicitor) for the trustees. They asked him to arrange the sale of four houses. He sold the houses to his brother, with whom he had made a prior arrangement that he would put up half the purchase price in return for two of the houses. When the trustees discovered this they sought to rescind the contract. W claimed specific performance but the House of Lords held that the contract was invalid and it was immaterial that the contract price was a fair one. Lord Blackburn said:

> "[W]e do not inquire whether it was a good bargain or a bad bargain before we set it aside. The mere fact that the agent was in

circumstances which made it his duty to give his client advice puts him in such a position that, being a purchaser himself, he cannot give disinterested advice—his own interests coming into contact with his client's; that mere fact authorises the client to set aside the contract, if he chooses so to do."

In a situation like *Armstrong* the agent will have to show that there was not a conflict of interest. This will usually be difficult and the onus will be on the agent to do so. In *Rigg's Executrix v. Urquhart* (1902) two brothers had entered into an agreement with their solicitor which conferred "a substantial benefit on him" with "little liability", over investment in a colliery. Lord Stormonth Darling came to the decision that, although the proposal had not been of the solicitor's making and he had acted throughout in a straightforward and honest manner, he still found in favour of the pursuers and had the agreement reduced. He quoted Lord Young in *Cleland v. Morrison* (1878): "'It is a rule that a solicitor taking a conveyance from his client in his own favour ought to see that the client's interests are in charge of another and independent solicitor. This is the rule and the practice of every solicitor who acts properly.'"

If the principal is aware of the possibility of a conflict of interest and continues with the contract, the principal will be barred from later rescinding the contract. This can be seen in *Harrods Ltd v. Lemon* (1931) where Lemon was selling a house using the services of the pursuer. She discovered that a potential (and ultimate) purchaser had used the services of a surveyor employed by the pursuers. This was clearly a conflict of interest Although Lemon expressed her dissatisfaction she allowed the sale to proceed. She then refused to pay the commission due on the sale on the ground that there had been a conflict of interest. It was held that she had to pay because she was aware of the conflict. This is no more than the operation of personal bar.

In *Kelly v. Cooper* (above at 27) the issue of conflict of interest was discussed at some length. It was said that where estate agents are concerned, it is their business to act for numerous principals. Where properties are of a similar description there will be a conflict of interest between the principals, each of whom will be concerned to attract potential purchasers to their property rather than that of another. Despite this conflict of interest, estate agents must be free to be act for several competing principals—otherwise they will be unable to perform their function as they could only ever sell one house at a time. In such cases there must be an implied term that the agent is free to act for other principals.

---

5. THE RELATIONSHIP BETWEEN AGENT, PRINCIPAL AND THIRD PARTY

The function of the agent is to link his principal and the third party in a contractual relationship which will impose rights and obligations on each of them. The agent should normally obtain no rights and have no obligations imposed on him under the contract. He will have, as it were, dropped out of the picture. He may incur liability to the third party, however, if he has been fraudulent or negligent, irrespective of whether the fraud or negligence was authorised by the principal or whether the principal has been bound.

The principal may also be liable for losses caused by the agent's fraud if the fraudulent act is within the agent's apparent authority. In *Lloyd v. Grace, Smith & Co.* (1912), the defendants were a firm of solicitors who had given their managing clerk, S, general authority to conduct the conveyancing business of the firm. S fraudulently induced the plaintiff, a widow, to make over some property to him and he sold it for his own benefit. It was held that the solicitors were liable to her because it was quite clear that the transaction (albeit for a fraudulent purpose) was one which was clearly within the apparent authority of a managing clerk.

AGENT'S AUTHORITY

The agent's authority to act on his principal's behalf is central to the whole idea of agency. It is this authority (or at least the aura of such authority) that empowers the agent to act on his principal's behalf and it is upon this authority that the third party will rely. This will obviously not be the case where the name or existence of the principal is not known (see Chapter 5).

Actual Authority
The actual authority of the agent covers both that authority which the agent has been given expressly by the principal and that which is implied from the position he holds.

Express Authority
Whether or not an agent succeeds in linking principal and third party in a contractual relationship will depend to a large extent on whether the agent has exceeded the authority given by his principal. If that authority has been exceeded, the principal will not be bound and the agent will be liable to the third party for breach of warranty of authority (See *J.M. & J. H. Robertson v. Beatson McLeod & Co.* (1908) where a chartered accountant who had been appointed to carry out a merger and had employed a solicitor to carry out some of the legal work was held to have exceeded his authority and was therefore personally liable to pay the solicitor's account.) In such cases, as we have seen earlier (see Chapter 1), the principal may choose to ratify the agent's unauthorised act; thus relieving the agent of liability. The authority possessed by the agent will, if disputed, be a question of fact in each case. The authority possessed by the agent may be expressly specified in the contract between them. When this is the case the agent's authority will usually be laid down clearly and concisely. Examples would be the detailed authority granted in deeds of power of attorney and in deeds of appointment of factors.

In most commercial agencies, if there is a dispute about the extent of the agent's powers, the courts will examine the type of agency involved, the relationship of the parties and other relevant circumstances such as trade custom in deciding what authority the agent is deemed to have.

Implied Authority
In addition to actual authority which is authority expressly conferred either in writing or orally, the agent has implied authority to do anything necessary for, or ordinarily incidental to, the carrying out of his duties. General agents have the implied authority that is generally recognised in their particular trade, business or profession. For example, a ship's captain has implied authority to employ a shipbroker and an architect in certain circumstances has implied authority to employ a surveyor (see above at 24). However, that authority is limited to what is necessary or expected: for example, a general agent has no implied power to borrow money. In *Sinclair, Moorhead & Co. v. Wallace & Co.* (1880) Lord Young said that the power to borrow money was a very important one and that it should be given expressly and within certain limits. No prudent money lender would be likely to lend money to an agent without seeing his authority to borrow and satisfying himself that the demand is within the prescribed borrowing limits.

An example of the danger facing an imprudent lender can be seen in *Paterson Brothers v. Gladstone* (1891). The pursuer partnership had three partners; the business was financially sound. The contract of co-partners provided that one of them had sole authority to handle the firm's financial affairs. One of the partners borrowed money (allegedly on the firm's behalf) at a rate of interest that far exceeded that usually applicable at that time. He embezzled the money. The court held that the firm was not liable to repay the money. While there was no doubt that borrowing money was within the ostensible authority of a partner, the court held that the partner's willingness to borrow at such high interest should have made the lenders suspicious and led them to make inquiries. The implied authority of a solicitor will depend on the circumstances. In *Riverford Finance Ltd v. Kelly* (1991) it was held that where a solicitor raised an action on his client's behalf he had implied authority to take an appeal to a higher court. However, it would seem from *Stephen v. Skinner* (1863) that a solicitor does not have implied authority to defend a case which goes to a higher court on appeal. A solicitor also has implied authority to abandon or compromise an action whether or not his client has authorised him to do so (*Mackenzie (Carpenters) Ltd (in receivership) v. Mowat* (1991)). It would seem from *Peden v. Graham* (1907) that a solicitor has no implied authority to accept repayments of the capital of a loan made by his principal. Nor in *Peden* was the agent held to have ostensible authority (see below).

Another example of implied authority can be seen in *Hely-Hutchinson v. Brayhead Ltd* (1968) where Lord Denning said that when the board of directors of a company appointed one of their number to be managing director they "thereby impliedly authorise him to do all such things as fall within the usual scope of that office". (In *Hely* there had in fact been no formal appointment of a managing director but the chairman acted as *de facto* managing director.) What may be done will, of course, depend upon the precise circumstances of each individual case. However, holding a particular position will, it seems, cloak an agent in a particular aura of implied authority. In *Watteau v. Fenwick* (1893) the owner of a pub sold it to a brewery company but stayed on as manager. He held the licence and his name was displayed above the door. The brewery bought all the goods for the pub except bottled beer and mineral water which the manager was authorised to buy. Watteau had supplied the manager with goods on credit, unaware that he was not the owner of the pub. When the manager failed to pay for a supply of cigars and Bovril, Watteau discovered the true position. It was held that the brewery were liable, although the manager had quite clearly acted outside his actual authority. Lord Coleridge said that "the principal is liable for all the acts of the agent which are within the authority usually confided to an agent of that character, notwithstanding limitations, as between the principal and the agent put upon that authority". As ordering the goods concerned would normally be within the authority of a pub manager, the principal was liable.

In contrast to *Watteau*, in *Daw v. Simmins* (1879) the facts were similar, but the third party was aware that the pub was "tied" to a brewery and therefore that the manager would be limited to buying spirits from nominees of the brewery. The brewery were, unlike the brewery in *Watteau*, not liable for the manager's actions. It would therefore seem that for implied authority to exist, there must be: (a) an agency already in existence, and (b) the type of relationship from which it is possible to work out what powers the agent will usually have.

It is obviously the latter that explains the different decisions in *Watteau* and *Daw*.

Ostensible (or Apparent) Authority

Another type of authority is ostensible or apparent authority. This is authority which has been neither expressly nor impliedly conferred but which the agent appears to have because of the conduct of principal and agent and the representation by the principal that the agent is acting on his behalf. An example can be seen in *Hayman v. American Cotton Oil Co.* (1907) where the defenders, a firm of oil merchants in America, in advertisements and letters to prospective customers represented that one McNairn of Glasgow was their exclusive agent in Great Britain. Ferguson & Co. of Glasgow bought oil from McNairn, paid in full but did not receive the goods. McNairn became bankrupt and an action of multiplepoinding (an action to ascertain ownership of goods where there are competing claims) was raised to ascertain the ownership of oil held in storage by the pursuers. The court held that the defenders had held out that McNairn was their agent "in quite distinct terms, and without any qualification whatever" and were therefore barred from denying the fact of McNairn's agency. (In the event, because of the particular circumstance of the case, the court held that a party who had dealt with McNairn had not dealt with him as agent.) The doctrine of personal bar by holding out operated here because it was believed that the third party either knew that the agent did not in fact have the apparent authority or could be taken as knowing that the authority was lacking.

Where the third party knows that the agent would not normally have authority, but he chooses to rely on the agent's (false) assertions that he does have authority, the principal will not be bound. This was what ultimately happened in *Hayman*, where it was held that as one of the parties dealing with McNairn knew that the transaction was not one which would have been authorised by the principal, or at least not on the terms agreed, the principal was not bound (but see below). It may be, for example, that a principal has withdrawn actual authority from an agent, but has failed to notify third parties of this, or that a principal has placed some restriction on an agent but has not made this known to third parties. In both these situations, the third party (unless aware of the reality) is justified in believing that the agent has the necessary authority to act on the principal's behalf. Statutory applications of ostensible authority can be seen in the Partnership Act 1890, s. 36(1) and the Factors (Scotland) Act 1890, s. 2(1).

In *Freeman & Lockyer (A Firm) v. Buckhurst Park Properties (Mangal) Ltd* (1964), Lord Diplock said: "'ostensible' authority, on the other hand, is a legal relationship between the principal and the contractor created by a representation, made by the principal to the contractor, intended to be and in fact acted upon by the contractor, that the agent has authority to enter on behalf of the principal into a contract of the kind within the scope of the "apparent' authority, so as to render the principal liable to perform any obligations imposed upon him by such contract ... and it is upon the apparent authority of the agent that the contractor normally relies in the ordinary course of business". In *Freeman & Lockyer* the plaintiffs were architects who had carried out work for the defendants on the instructions of one Kapoor, who was one of three directors of the defendants. Kapoor was not the managing director but the other two directors allowed him to act as if he were. The plaintiffs sued the company for their fees (Kapoor having vanished). The company argued that Kapoor was not managing director and had not been authorised to act on behalf of the company. It was held that by not intervening when they knew that Kapoor was acting as if he were managing director, they had held him out to be managing director. It was within the ostensible authority of a managing director to enter into contracts and therefore the company was bound. What is clear from *Freeman* is that the representation or holding out includes omission as well as commission.

Two recent English cases would seem to indicate a division of opinion by the judiciary where ostensible authority is concerned. The cases *Armagas v. Mundogas SA (The Ocean Frost)* (1986) and *First Energy (U.K.) Ltd v. Hungarian International Bank* (1993) are analysed by Reynolds in (1994) 110 L.Q.R. 21, at pp. 23–25. In *Armagas* the House of Lords restated the principle that where the third party knows that the agent would not normally have the authority and there is nothing beyond the agent's own false assertion to indicate that he has authority, then the principal is not bound. In *Armagas*, Mundogas were trying to sell one of their ships. Their vice president and chartering manager, Magelssen, used the services of Johannsen, a partner in a firm of shipbrokers, to arrange the sale. Armagas expressed an interest, but only if Mundogas would charter the vessel back for three years. Mundogas had no interest in such an arrangement. However, Magelssen, who had no authority to conclude such a deal, conspired with Johannsen as part of a fraudulent scheme to have Armagas believe that Magelssen had been given specific authority to effect such a sale and charter back. The appropriate documents were signed. Due to external circumstances the scheme collapsed and Armagas sued Mundogas on the basis of the three-year contract. The House of Lords held the view that Magelssen's position could not be taken as giving him ostensible authority to enter into such a contract. Ostensible authority could only arise if the representation came from the principal (see *Freeman & Lockyer* above). The only representations as to authority came from the co-conspirators Magelssen and Johannsen. Lord Keith said: "No representation by Mr. Magelssen can help Armagas. It must be in a position to found on some relevant representation by the responsible management of Mundogas as to Mr. Magelssen's authority." As Armagas were unable to do so their action failed.

However, in *First Energy (U.K.) Ltd*, the court held that where the agent (a bank manager) had no authority to grant a loan and the third party knew this, an offer of such a loan was binding on the principal (the bank). The reasoning in *First Energy* seems to be that although the manager lacked the authority to grant the loan, he had been put into a position where he would normally communicate head office approval of loans. Lord Stein said:

> "[his] position as senior manager ... was such that he was clothed with ostensible authority to communicate that head office approval had been granted ... the idea that the [plaintiffs] should have checked with the managing director in London whether the bank had approved the transaction seems unreal. In my judgement a decision that [the manager] did not have apparent authority to communicate head office approval would defeat the reasonable expectations of the parties and it would fly in the face of the way practice negotiations are conducted between trading banks and trading customers."

The court had to uphold the "reasonable business expectations of honest men".

In *Dornier GmbH v. Cannon* (1991), there was a dispute whether a sum of money paid by the pursuers to the defender was a loan, as the pursuers contended, or a grant. The defender's claim that the money advanced was a grant was based on the existence of back letters from the pursuers to the defender which negated any obligation in relation to the purported loan. The back letter had been signed on the pursuer's behalf by two of their employees. The defender claimed the back letter was a forgery and even if it was not the employees had not been authorised to bind them other than in terms of the loan agreement.

Lord Hope said that the more extraordinary the transaction then the less likely it was that the agent had authority to enter into it. It would be a question of fact and degree as to whether the agent's actions were within his apparent or ostensible authority. (See also Brown, "Agent's Apparent Authority: Paradigm or Paradox" (1995) J.B.L. 360.)

Further illustrations of what constitutes ostensible authority can be seen in the following cases. In *International Sponge Importers v. Watt and Sons* (1911) the pursuers employed a commercial traveller, Cohen. He sold sponges to the defenders. Invoices issued by the pursuers stated that the only acceptable means of payment was by crossed cheque made out to themselves. However, on at least one occasion payment was made by open cheque in Cohen's name without the pursuers objecting. Cohen and two colleagues subsequently devised a fraudulent scheme whereby he persuaded the defender to pay him either by cheque made out to himself or in gold and notes, and his colleagues covered this up in the accounts. Cohen, of course, embezzled these monies. When the fraud came to light the pursuers being unable to recover the money from Cohen, who had made himself scarce, sought to recover the sum defrauded from the defenders. They failed. The deciding factor seemed to have been that in spite of the fact that the pursuers' invoices asked for crossed cheques in their favour, this had never been expressly intimated to the defenders. The fact that on at least one occasion no objection was made when the cheque for payment was made out to Cohen was also a crucial factor, although the pursuers were unaware of this as Cohen's colleagues had managed to conceal the fact.

In *British Bata Shoe Company v. Double M. Shah* (1981) the pursuers' cashier had devised a fraudulent scheme whereby cheques for goods sold were to be sent to him with the payee's name left blank. The defenders agreed to this somewhat unusual method of payment and, surprise, surprise, the cashier embezzled the money. The pursuers, relying on the principle of ostensible authority which had been successfully put forward in *International Sponge Importers*, sued the defenders for payment. However, they were unsuccessful. Lord Jauncey said that *International Sponge Importers* rested on its own facts. He quoted Bowstead on *Agency* on when an agent with ostensible authority binds his principal:

"'Where a person by words or conduct represents or permits it to be represented that another person had authority to act on his own behalf, he is bound by the acts of such other person with respect to any person dealing with him as an agent in good faith of any such representation, to the same extent as if such other person had the authority that he was represented to have even although he had no actual authority.'"

The court in *Bata* were of the view that the way in which payment was to be made should have put the third party on inquiry. This had not been an issue in *International Sponge Importers* because of the more sophisticated nature of the fraud.

In *Rama Corporation Ltd v. Proved Tin and General Investments Ltd* (1952), Slade J. said that there were three requirements for ostensible authority to exist. These requirements are not different in any major sense from those laid down in other cases involving ostensible authority but have the advantage of brevity. They were: (a) a representation; (b) a reliance on the representation; and (c) an alteration of a party's position resulting from such reliance. All these are present in *Hayman*. In *Freeman & Lockyer* the "representation" was in the non-intervention of the other directors. In *Armagas* there was a representation, but this is not enough. The

representation must come from the principal. In *Armagas* it came from the
agent. The three requirements of Slade J. can usefully be applied to the
other cases discussed above. In *George v. Duncan* (1991) a taxi driver
employed by a firm put his taxi into a garage for repair. The taxi carried the
firm's sign. It was held that the sign gave the driver ostensible authority to
enter on behalf of the firm a contract for repairs to the vehicle. The sign
was the representation, relying on which the garage carried out the repairs
to the car. The firm was therefore liable for the cost of the repairs.

There may well be confusion as to whether the agent has implied actual
authority or ostensible authority. This confusion is not limited to students.
In *Hely-Hutchinson v. Brayhead* (above), at first instance, Roskill J. treated
the case as one involving ostensible authority while in the Court of Appeal
it was treated as one involving implied authority.

The case of *Waugh v. Clifford* (1982) attempts to draw a clear distinction
between implied authority and ostensible authority. It used the example of a
defence solicitor in a defamation action who makes the plaintiff's solicitor a
very high settlement offer. It is quite clear, said Brightman J., that the defence
solicitor has ostensible authority to do this. It does not, however, follow that
he would have implied authority to do so without consulting the client. In
Brightman's view a clear distinction has to be drawn between the ostensible
authority the solicitor has *vis-à-vis* the third party and the implied authority
he has *vis-à-vis* his client. Stone makes the point (*Law of Agency*, p. 44) that
while it is quite clear from this case that the implied authority existing between
principal and agent may often be co-terminous with the agent's ostensible
authority they are not one and the same.

Another type of authority is presumed authority which is the authority
which the law presumes the principal would have given had he been
consulted. Many cases of presumed authority revolved around the presumed
authority of a wife to order goods for the household for which her husband
would be liable to pay. The law, however, changed in 1984 and the presumed
authority of spouses is no longer an issue, although the reader may still
come across cases involving implied or ostensible authority of spouses. An
example of presumed authority is s. 35 of the Companies Act 1985. Agency
of necessity is no more than an example of presumed authority.

---

6. AGENT'S LIABILITY

Agents are liable to indemnify their principals if they have acted outwith
their actual authority. In addition, if agents acting beyond their authority
have made a contract with a third party, which their principal refuses to
ratify, they will be liable to the third party for breach of warranty of authority.

Whether agents have exceeded their authority or not they may still incur
liability in certain circumstances. Liability (if any) will depend on how the
agent has contracted with the third party. The agent may have disclosed the
fact of his agency and either named his principal or refused to name him

(often one of the reasons for using agents is anonymity), or the agent may not have disclosed the fact of his agency at all.

Where the agent has acted fraudulently, the principal will not be liable unless he has made the fraud possible or has benefited from it. The same principle has been held to apply where the agent deliberately failed to communicate material facts to his principal: *Muir's Executors v. Craig's Trustees* (1913), where a solicitor agent had forged his aunt's signature on a bond and disposition and embezzled the money advanced. When she received a bill from the Inland Revenue for tax due on the bond, knowing that she had no such bond she sent another nephew to inquire at the tax offices. He discovered the existence of the fraud but did not, at his brother's request, inform his aunt of the forgery. The issue before the court was whether she was barred from challenging the bond due to her agent's (second nephew's) knowledge of the fraud. Lord President Dunedin said that he could "not help but call such an argument an absurdity". In Lord Mackenzie's judgment the second nephew was no more than "a messenger" and he seems to have doubted the existence of any agency between the aunt and the second nephew in any case, referring as he does to the so-called agency here. However, where the agent has misrepresented the true position, the principal may have to bear the loss for the agent's defaults even although the principal has attempted to limit the agent's authority "to the collection of monthly subscriptions". (*Laing v. Provincial Homes* (1909)). In *Laing* the pursuer had allegedly been induced to enter into the contract through the defender's agent's misrepresentation to her. She sought to rescind the contract. The court said that the company could not on the one hand say "they will not be liable for the misstatements of agents, and yet be able to keep the contract which the misstatements of the agents procured".

Agent for named principal

As a general rule the agent will incur no liability and has no title to sue on the contract. There are, however, some exceptions to this:

(a) where the agent expressly and in writing incurs liability. In *Stewart v. Shannessy* (1900) the court quoted with approval the English case of *Thomson v. Davenport* (1829) where it was held that where a person signs a contract in his own name he is prima facie deemed to be a person contracting personally. To avoid this situation the agent must always make it clear that he is merely an agent and incurs no personal liability. The normal way to do this is for the agent to include after his signature the words "as agent", "on behalf of principal" or "for and on behalf of". In *Stone & Rolfe Ltd v. Kimber Coal Co. Ltd* (1926) a charterparty for the carriage of coal had been signed on behalf of the charterers by their agents. The contract was signed "for" (the charterers). The owner of the ship subsequently sued the charterers' agents for various expenses. It was held that the form of signature by the agents made it quite clear that they were signing as agents only. However, in the Court of Session the judges had held that the form of signature was not enough to relieve the agents of liability. They felt the words "as agents" should have been added. (See also *Digby Brown & Co. v. Lyall* (1995) where a letter of obligation granted by a firm of solicitors "on behalf of" their clients, but signed by them without qualification, was not binding on the firm personally.) Care should be taken, however, by agents lest they are held liable in such situations. In *Stone & Rolfe* the use of the words "for the" was enough to exempt them from liability, the existence of the principal had been named and disclosed and liability fell upon him. However, in *Stewart v. Shannessy* (1900) it was held that the proper construction of the document under dispute was that the agent was liable. Shannessy, who was sales agent for two companies, appointed Stewart as a representative of the companies. In the letter of appointment, which was on one of the companies' headed notepaper, Shannessy signed the letter in his own name with no indication that he was an agent. In a dispute over payment of commission it was held that Shannessy was liable as there had been no indication that he was merely acting as agent. Particular care should be taken by an agent signing a negotiable instrument. It would seem that if he wishes to avoid liability he should make it absolutely clear that he is signing as an agent. The mere addition of "as agent" will not be enough. He should make it clear that he is signing for or on behalf of a principal. In *Brebner v. Henderson* (1925) it was held that where a promissory note was signed "James Gordon Director, Alex Henderson Secretary, The Fraserburgh Empire Ltd", this was not sufficient to exempt the two signatories from personal liability. The reason for this decision (and others) would seem to be that the courts have drawn a distinction between words following a signature which are merely descriptive of the signatory and words which indicate the capacity in which the signatory signs. The distinction is arguably a very fine one (see Bills of Exchange Act 1882, s. 26(i)). It is clear from *Lord Advocate v. Chung* (see Chapter 1) that signing "as representative" will not relieve the agent of personal liability;

(b) where his personal liability is implied by the custom of a particular trade, *e.g.* the personal liability of law agents for charges which by the custom of their profession are usually paid by them, such as an account for printing (*Neill & Co. v. Hopkirk* (1850)). Other examples involving liability arising from custom and trade in the legal profession are the solicitor's liability for the expenses of a witness (*McDonald v. Meldrum* (1839)), the fees of an advocate's clerk (*Fortune's Executors v. Smith* (1864)) and the liability of a solicitor for sheriff officers' poinding fees (*Stirling Park & Co. v. Digby Brown & Co.* (1995)). In *Pike v. Ongley* (1887) it was demonstrated to the court's satisfaction that there was a custom in the hop trade that where an agent does not identify his principal at the time of contracting then the agent himself will be personally liable;

(c) where the principal has no contractual capacity, *e.g.* a contract made on behalf of an unincorporated body which has no separate legal personality (see *McMeekin v. Easton*, below) or the "principal" in an as yet unregistered company (see *Kelner v. Baxter*, above at 11 and, generally, below at 44).

Agent for an unnamed principal
This is an area where there is little Scottish authority and which is not particularly clear in England. Bowstead suggests that whatever the rule is,

it ought to be that the agent should be liable alongside the principal. Normally the same general principles apply as apply where the principal is named. There is, however, a presumption that the third party would have been unwilling to contract with someone whose identity was unknown to him. As a result, the personal liability of the agent will be more readily inferred in construing the contract but this will depend upon the exact circumstances of the case.

In *Ferrier v. Dods* (1865) Lord President Inglis was of the opinion that an auctioneer "who warrants the thing he sells without disclosing the name of the principal is personally liable for the warranty" (see also below at 43). If there is no such warranty then presumably there will be no such personal liability. An auctioneer who gives a warranty will not, however, be liable where he has been authorised to do so and the identity of the seller is known. As far as the general issue of an auctioneer's liability is concerned, the English case of *Payne v. Leconfield* (1882) suggests that an auctioneer does not warrant the goods sold.

The agent may be liable by trade usage or custom or, Gow has suggested (at p. 524), because he does not name his principal within a certain time or within a reasonable time. The case Gow relies on is *J and J Brydon v. Muir* (1869). It seems clear from the case, however, that the agent's liability arose because he did not disclose the name of the *third party* to the principal, thus making it impossible for the principal to recover money owed. In *The Santa Carina* (1971) it was held that even if a trade custom can make the agent personally liable, the custom's existence has to be proved. This case involved a telephone order placed between two brokers. Both were aware that the other was unlikely to be acting on his own behalf although this was not discussed by them. Lord Denning said:

"I know that in many trades there is a custom by which the broker is liable. Those cases rest on a custom of the trade. There was no such custom alleged or proved [in this case]. It seems to me that, in the circumstances of this case, the proper inference is that the agents were, when they gave the telephone message, giving it as agents only."

Where the agent has contracted on behalf of an unnamed principal, and in the absence of any liability as discussed above, the third party if sued by the principal cannot plead compensation of a debt owed to him by the agent. In *Matthews v. Auld & Guild* (1873) Matthews had instructed Henderson, a Dundee stockbroker, to carry out a transaction for him. Henderson used the defenders, Glasgow stockbrokers, to effect the transaction. They knew Henderson was acting on a client's behalf. Henderson subsequently absconded owing a large sum of money to Auld & Guild. They sought to retain money they held as a result of the transaction carried out by Henderson on Matthews' behalf. The court held that they could not plead compensation as they knew that Henderson was acting as an agent.

However, where the agent has acted for a principal whose existence was not disclosed, the third party may plead compensation of a debt owed to him by the agent provided that the debt was incurred before the third party came to know of the principal's existence (*Wester Moffat Colliery Co. v. Jeffrey* (1911)).

Principal undisclosed
Where the agent acts for an undisclosed principal, both principal and agent
are liable. This liability is alternative, not joint and several. The third party
will obviously first look to the agent for performance and hold him liable
for breach. The principal may, however, disclose himself (or be disclosed)
and is then liable. In *Bennett v. Inveresk Paper Co.* (1891) the pursuer had
ordered newsprint through his London agent. The paper mill did not know
of Bennett's existence. Upon the arrival in Australia, the paper was found
to be faulty. Bennett's attempt to sue for breach was resisted by the paper
company on the ground that where there was a contract between a seller in
the United Kingdom and a purchaser abroad which was effected through
an agent it was a presumption of law that the middleman agent contracted
as an independent contracting party with the seller and the ultimate purchaser
respectively and that as a matter of law the intermediary could be the agent
of either party. If there was no agency, Bennett would have no title to sue
Inveresk. Lord McLaren found that although this might be the rule
sometimes, it was clearly not the intention of the parties in this case. This
being the case, the normal rules regarding undisclosed principals should
apply. He said there was no doubt "that a seller to the agent of an undisclosed
principal, when he comes to know the name of the principal, may elect to
sue the principal for the price. Correspondingly the principal ... may come
forward and disclose himself, and may sue the other party in his own name".
Whether or not he will be successful will depend on the circumstances.

   In *Lavaggi v. Pirie & Sons* (1872) the pursuers sent rags to one Wood for
resale. He sold them to Pirie without disclosing the fact that he was an
agent. Woods had dealt with the defenders, as principal, on many previous
occasions. Woods became insolvent, owing Pirie more than the value of
the rags. The existence of the pursuers as principal only emerged after
Woods' bankruptcy. The court held that the pursuers could not recover the
value of the rags from Pirie, because by the time their existence as principal
was disclosed it was too late, as the agent (Woods) was already bankrupt.
Fatal to the pursuers' case was Lord Moncrieff's view that Woods had all
along acted as principal.

   In *Armstrong v. Stokes* (1872), Blackburn J. said:
      "[I]t is too firmly established that where a person employs another to
      make a contract for him, he as principal is liable to the seller, although
      the seller had never heard of his existence and entered into the contract
      solely on the credit of the person whom he believed to be the principal
      though in fact he was not. It is established law that if on the failure of
      the person with whom the vendor believed himself to be contracting,
      the vendor discovers there is an undisclosed principal behind, he is
      entitled to take advantage of this unexpected godsend."
This view has recently been echoed in the House of Lords by Lord Jauncey
in *Boyter v. Thomson* (1995). The defender was the owner of a cabin cruiser
and he instructed a yacht broker to sell it on his behalf. The pursuer bought
the boat but later discovered that it had defects which rendered her
unseaworthy and amounted to breaches of the seller's implied obligations
under the Sale of Goods Act 1979. When he bought the boat the pursuer

believed it belonged to the brokers. The defender argued that the relevant section of the legislation did not apply to him as it only applied to the obligations owed by agents where they acted for an undisclosed principal, and the correct interpretation of the section was that only the agent was liable. This argument was rejected by Lord Jauncey on behalf of the House. He said this was an incorrect interpretation and that the normal common law rules applied and the principal could be sued on any contract made on his behalf.

Whether or not there will be a duty on the third party to inquire as to the existence of an undisclosed principal will depend on a variety of factors. A third party who should inquire and neglects to do so may lose the right to set off the agent's debt to him. It is difficult to find a consistent principle from the decisions. In *Lavaggi* (above) it was held that there was no duty to inquire as to whether there was a principal, even although Pirie knew the rags had been supplied by someone else. However, in *Lavaggi* there had been a long course of dealing between Woods and Pirie as principals. In *Armour v. Duff* (1912), however, it was held that due to the nature of the shipping business there was an obligation to discover whether there was a principal and indeed this was something which could easily be established by examining the Register of Shipping.

Election between principal and agent when principal undisclosed
The third party will have to choose whether to sue the agent or the principal but cannot, as the liability is alternative, choose to sue both. Both Walker and Markesinis and Munday agree that the third party's first recourse is against the agent but once the existence and identity of the principal is made known, the third party has the right to elect whether he wishes to hold agent or principal liable. In *Ferrier v. Dodds* the court pointed out (somewhat unnecessarily) that election cannot arise until the name of the undisclosed principal is known. Once he has made the choice it is final (*Ferrier v. Dodds* (1865)). In *Ferrier* the defender was an auctioneer who had sold to Ferrier a horse which he warranted to be a good worker. Ferrier claimed that the horse was unfit and this was accepted by Dodds who asked him to return the mare to B, its former owner. Ferrier did so, and then sued both B and Dodds. It was held that by returning the mare to B, Ferrier was deemed to have elected to sue him and could not also sue Dodds. Lord President Inglis said:

> "He [the buyer] was entitled to go against Dodds as seller because the principal had not been originally disclosed, or against the true owner now disclosed. But he was not entitled to go against both. What the law gave him was an election or option. He went on to say that Ferrier was only entitled to get his money back if he returned the mare, and the only person from whom he was entitled to get the money was the person to whom he had returned it."

For the right to election to exist it will have to be established that there was an agency relationship in the first place and that the agent acted within his authority because, as Gloag on *Contract* says (at page 143), an undisclosed principal cannot ratify his agent's unauthorised acts. The consequences of this would be that if there can be no ratification in such circumstances, there will be no agency and therefore the "purported" principal will be unable to sue or be sued on the contract, and the question of election will not arise. As we saw above (at 12), this view may not be correct.

In England if the third party sues the agent to judgment this amounts to an election and will prevent the third party later suing the undisclosed principal (*Kendall v. Hamilton* (1879)). In *Craig v. Blackater* (1923), Craig had supplied Blackater with two ship's boilers. Blackater failed to pay the full price and Craig sued. Blackater claimed that the boilers were not conform to contract and counterclaimed. It emerged during pleadings that Blackater was not the owner of the ship for whom the boilers were ordered but merely the managing agent for the Cadeby Steamship Co. Ltd. Craig maintained the action against Blackater but in the counterclaim Craig argued that Blackater had no title to sue as any loss suffered had been by Cadeby, not Blackater. The court held that by Craig suing Blackater to decree they had elected to treat Blackater as the debtor and therefore the counterclaim was competent. Sheriff McEwan says in *Stair Memorial Encyclopaedia,* Vol. 1 at para. 657 that the decision has always been considered good law (and has indeed been followed). Moreover, he suggests that if the principal's right to counterclaim through his agent was recognised as good it would be hard to justify refusing an action against him if the agent was unable to pay. He admits that this would be a departure from the normal alternative liability but says that exceptions to the rule have been made such as *Lamont, Nisbett & Co. v. Hamilton* (1907) where Lord McLaren felt that it was obvious from provisions of the contract between agent (which were not disclosed to the principal) and third party that the third party elected to take the agent as sole debtor and that there was consequently no question of alternative liability. In *Meier and Co. v. Kuchenmeister* (1881) the court held there was a form of joint liability. Sheriff McEwan feels that "there is no good reason in logic or equity why the anomaly of the undisclosed principal should be treated the same".

Agent for non-existent principal
There are two possibilities here. It may be that there is in fact no "principal" at all; the agent is acting on his own behalf. The other more usual possibility is where the agent contracts as agent but his "principal" is not yet in existence. This would be the situation where a company is in the process of formation (see *Kelner v. Baxter*, above at 11 where it was held that the defendant who had acted on behalf of an as yet unregistered company was personally liable on the contract). The company for which the "agent" purported to act will also be unable to enforce the contract. In *Tinnevelley Sugar Refining Co v. Mirrlees, Watson and Yaryan* (above at 11) when the company attempted to sue on a contract entered into by its promoters it was held that it could not do so. The company was, Lord Robertson said, in an untenable position.

A Scottish company might plead a *jus quaesitum tertio* (third party right) on a pre-incorporation contract of the type in *Kelner* and *Tinnevelley*. This was confirmed in *Cumming v. Quartzag Ltd* (1981), in which the Inner

House recognised the plea as relevant (although it failed on the facts). In order to succeed with such a plea it would appear that the promoter would have had to sign the pre-incorporation contract as principal rather than as a purported agent of the company, and the contract would have to provide expressly in favour of the yet-to-be-formed company.

This requirement may now, however, arguably be redundant by virtue of s. 36C of the Companies Act 1985 which re-implements part of the first EC Company Law Directive. It states:

> "where a contract purports to be made by a company, or by a person as agent for a company, at a time when the company has not yet been formed, then subject to any agreement to the contrary, the contract shall have effect as a contract entered into by the person purporting to act for the company or as agent for it, and he shall be personally liable on the contract accordingly."

The effect of this provision is that in a *Kelner v. Baxter* situation the person making the contract will be personally liable on it. It should be noted, however, that the section only applies where there is no "agreement to the contrary". The parties involved may choose to arrange for some alternative distribution of liabilities. If there is any "agreement to the contrary" it must be clearly stated for it to be effective (*Phonogram v. Lane* (1981)). The section makes no mention of the agent's right to enforce the contract against the third party. In *Newborne v. Sensolid* (1954), an agent who purported to contract on behalf of an as yet unformed company was held to have no title to sue on the contract. This is likely no longer to be the case. Fridman and Bowstead both suggest that the correct interpretation of s 36(4) is that the agent will be able to enforce a contract.

Another example is where the "principal" has no legal personality, *e.g.* a congregation or club. In *McMeekin v. Easton* (1889) a church member paid a debt owed by the minister and two of the office bearers "in the name and on behalf of" the church. The congregation agreed to meet this obligation but later changed its mind. The court held that as the congregation was not a person, it could not therefore take on the personal obligation of a debtor, and that the defenders were therefore liable.

Breach of warranty of authority

If an agent, purporting to act as such, exceeds both his actual and ostensible authority then he cannot effect a contract between the principal and third party—unless, of course, the principal chooses and is able to ratify the agent's actions. The agent may, however, be liable in damages to the third party not on the contract but on the ground that he had breached the implied collateral warranty of authority that he had authority to enter the contract on his principal's behalf. In *Anderson v. Croall* (1903), a horse was wrongly (but innocently) sold at auction. The true owner of the horse refused to hand over the horse because he had not authorised its sale. It was held that the unsuccessful purchaser was entitled to damages from the auctioneers for breach of warranty of authority. The sum of damages in *Anderson* included payment for lost profit on the resale of the horse at a later auction. If, however, it can be shown that the principal's obligation is worthless, *e.g.* because of insolvency, then there may be little point in raising an action.

In *Irving v. Burns* (1915) an agent who had no authority had instructed a plumber to carry out work. The principal, however, had no assets and the court held that the plumber had therefore not lost anything, and could not recover from the agent for breach of warranty of authority.

Where the agent's authority is a question of law and can be ascertained by the third party no liability for breach of warranty of authority will arise. In *Beattie v. Lord Ebury* (1874) it was held that the directors of a company which had no authority to borrow money were not liable on debentures which they had issued in the belief that they could do so. Whether there was a power to borrow was a question of law, not fact, and was one which could be ascertained by third parties. In *Firbank's Executors. v. Humphreys* (1886) where the directors had issued debentures in excess of the authorised limit they were liable, as the court held that whether the limit had been exceeded was a question of fact and not law. These decisions would now be subject to s. 35(1) of the Companies Act 1985.

The agent's liability for breach of warranty of authority has traditionally been held to arise only where the warranty was given to the third party who sought to deal with the principal. In *Penn v. Bristol Building Society* (1977) the issue arose as to whether the agent could be liable for breach of warranty of authority where the warranty was given to someone other than the third party. In *Penn* a solicitor acted in the sale of a house. He acted on behalf of the joint owner of the house, and believed he had the authority of the other joint owner. In fact he had no such authority. The sale was part of a fraud designed to raise money from the building society. The society lent money as the security of the house. When the second joint owner discovered the situation she obtained a declaration that the security was null and void. She also won damages against the solicitor. The building society also sued the solicitor for breach of warranty of authority and the court held that the solicitor's warranty had been given not only to the house purchaser (who was part of the fraudulent scheme) but also to the building society who relied on it when lending the money.

---

7. TERMINATION OF AGENCY

In the commercial world there will normally be a contract between principal and agent and in such circumstances the normal rules as to termination of contract will apply. The relationship between the principal and agent can be terminated in any of the following circumstances.

When the contract so provides

It may be the case that the contract of agency specifies that it is to terminate either upon the completion of a particular task or after the expiry of an agreed period of time. One issue that has arisen in several cases is whether or not the agent is entitled to any period of notice when the relationship is terminated. *Brenan v. Campbell's Trustees* (1895) is concerned with both the completion of a task and the expiry of an agreed time. Brenan had been an agent for Campbell for several years and in October 1890 he was appointed for a further period of four years upon the express provision that he employ a relative of Campbell as an apprentice. At the end of the four-year period (and of the apprenticeship) Brenan was informed that his services as agent would no longer be required. He claimed he was due six months' notice, arguing that the relationship between the parties was one of master and servant and that the fact that he had been engaged for a definite period made no difference. The Lord President (Robertson) found that Brenan was not a servant (employee) of the trustee "in the true sense of the terms" but of much greater significance was the fact that Brenan was employed under a very special contract—*i.e.* the duration of the contract was linked to the co-terminous apprenticeship. Indeed he saw the apprenticeship as the reason for the agency agreement. There may, however, be situations where the terms of the contract are not as clear as they were in *Brenan*.

In *Stevenson v. North British Ry* (1905) an agent who was in business in his own right was also employed as an agent for the railway company for the transportation of coal over their lines. The Lord Justice-Clerk felt that the arrangement was a "complex one" where arrangements had to be made not for the moment, but for a long period ahead. The agency was terminated on three months' notice. At the time of notice, however, the agent had effectively secured the principal's business for the coming year and in the circumstances the court held that he was entitled to rely on his agency being renewed for another year; it was difficult to see how any such business could be taken up by a prudent man, if it might be abruptly closed at any time.

Termination by principal or agent
If the contract of agency was silent as to duration, then either the principal or agent may terminate it at any time. The relationship depends upon common consent and can therefore be ended by such consent. In addition to termination by agreement, the relationship may also be terminated by the unilateral act of either principal or agent. Either party may at any time summarily terminate the agreement.

If the principal terminates the agency in such circumstances he is still under an obligation to pay the agent any remuneration that remains unpaid. He is also under a continuing obligation to indemnify the agent in respect of any liabilities incurred in the course of the agency. (See also Commercial Agents at Chapter 7). Where the principal terminates the agency, the agent will normally be allowed to complete any transactions in which he is engaged. The deciding factor will be whether the third party has acted to his prejudice in the belief that the agent–principal relationship still existed. It would not be possible, for example, to terminate an auctioneer's authority *vis-à-vis* a specific item after the item had been knocked down to a bidder. His authority to sell could, of course, be revoked at any time before the item was knocked down.

Upon termination of the agency the principal is allowed continuing access to the agent's records in so far as they relate to the principal's affairs and provided that such access has not been expressly excluded. In *Yasuda Fire and Marine Insurance v. Orion Marine Insurance* (1995), Colman J. found that there was a general duty on an agent to provide a principal with information, irrespective of any contractual provision. There was no reason, he said, why such a duty, which enables the principal to check on what has been done in his name, should terminate when the agency does.

Termination of agency must, of course, be communicated but the issue of whether "notice" (or how much notice) need be given may not be straightforward.

Agent appointed for a fixed term

An unjustified termination before the expiry of the fixed period will usually be a breach of contract which will leave the party terminating the agreement liable in damages. However, much will depend upon the wording of the contract. In *Rhodes v. Forwood* (1876) the agent was appointed for a seven-year period to sell any coal the principal might send from his coal mine. After four years the principal sold the mine. The agent claimed for loss of commission during the remaining three years. His claim was unsuccessful because there was no guarantee in the agency contract that the agreement would remain in force or that the principal would be in business for the seven years. In contrast, in *Turner v. Goldsmith* (1891) the agent was contracted to sell shirts "manufactured or sold" by the principal for a five-year period. The principal's factory was destroyed by fire before the expiry of the five years and the principal went out of business. The agent's claim for breach was upheld on the ground that the agreement was not limited to shirts manufactured in the now burnt-down factory.

A Scottish case where there was a similar issue to these cases was *Patmore & Co. v. Cannon & Co. Ltd* (1892) where Patmore agreed to act as sales agent for the defender's leather and other goods for a five-year period. A few months later Cannon informed Patmore that they were withdrawing from the leather goods business but were continuing to deal in dip and glue. They arranged to introduce Patmore to another firm who dealt in leather goods who were looking for an agent. Patmore refused this offer and sued Cannon for damages for breach of contract. Their claim was unsuccessful as the court found that Cannon had not bound itself to carry on its business or any part of it for five years (or any other period) simply for the benefit of Patmore. The decision of the House of Lords in *Rhodes* was referred to and followed by the judges in *Patmore* both at first instance and on appeal.

Agent appointed for indeterminate term

Where the agent is appointed for an indeterminate term there may, of course, be contractual provision as to notice. If the contract is silent as to notice— and terminating without such notice will amount to breach unless of course the principal is justified—reasonable notice will have to be given. What is reasonable will, of course, depend on the circumstances: *e.g.* it may be the case that inadequate notice will be severely prejudicial to the other party.

In *Martin-Baker Aircraft Co. Ltd v. Canadian Flight Equipment Ltd* (1955) the agent agreed to act as "sole selling agent" for the principal. He agreed actively to promote his principal's products, and not to sell those of competitors. The court held that there was a commercial relationship based on confidence and trust which was terminable on reasonable notice (reasonable notice in the circumstances being 12 months). Where the agent is an employee, statutory provisions as to notice will of course apply (Employment Rights Act 1996, s. 86).

There are circumstances where the agency is irrevocable unless reasonable cause can be shown for its revocation. This will be the case where the agent is a procurator *in rem suam* (for his own benefit) (known in England as an agent with authority coupled with an interest). An example of an irrevocable agency would be where the principal owes the agent money and gives him authority to sell some of the principal's property to pay the debt. However, if the principal authorises the agent to sell property, and the agent then lends the principal money, here the authority is not irrevocable. The agent must have the interest *when* the authority is granted.

Another example of procuratory *in rem suam* can be seen in the case of *Galbraith & Moorhead v. Arethusa Ship Co. Ltd* (1896) where the pursuers, who were ship brokers, agreed to take 500 shares in the defender company provided that they were appointed sole chartering brokers for the *Arethusa*. This was subject to the pursuers being able "to do as well as any other brokers regarding rates and terms". The defenders agreed. The agreement continued for several years until, following a change in the management of the defenders, the pursuers were no longer sole chartering brokers. They consequently raised an action against the defenders for damages. Their action succeeded. The Lord President (Robertson) held that while this could not be seen as a perpetual contract, the applicable conditions were the continued existence of the *Arethusa* (and of the pursuers) and the latter's ability to offer as good rates and terms as other brokers. Lord Adam further added that the case depended solely upon the construction of the agreement—the question was whether the agreement could be terminated by the defenders upon reasonable notice, or on reasonable cause only. Noting that the pursuers had paid for their appointment by the taking of 500 shares in the defender company, he held that he had great difficulty in holding that an agreement for which consideration (the 500 shares) had been given could be terminated at will by the other contracting party.

TERMINATION BY OPERATION OF LAW

Certain events will automatically terminate the agency whether or not the agent or principal wishes this to be the case.

Expiry of the relevant period of time

It may be that the agency has been expressed as lasting for a specific period. If this is the case it will automatically terminate at the end of that period. If there is no express period stated then one may be implied by trade custom. For example, the authority of a stockbroker (unless there is evidence otherwise), will be presumed to terminate at the end of the current account.

Purpose of the agency accomplished

If the agent has been authorised to act with regard to a specific piece of business, then once he has done this the agency is terminated. Thereafter he is what is known as *functus officio* (he has fulfilled his purpose). In *Blackburn v. Scholes* (1810) it was held that an agent, who had sold the goods for whose sale he had been employed, had no authority to agree to a subsequent alteration of the terms of sale. Once the sale had been completed his agency (and therefore authority) terminated. It might, of course, be the case that he retained ostensible authority (see above at 34).

FRUSTRATION OF THE AGENCY

The normal rules as to frustration of contract apply. It should be noted that if the agent is also an employee the courts will be reluctant to find frustration as it may deny the agent/employee his statutory rights. Some particular examples of frustration in agency include the following:

It may be the case that the agency was established for the sale or purchase of a specific item. If this is the case then the destruction, either actual or constructive, of the item will terminate the agency (see *Rhodes v. Forwood* at 48). Other examples of impossibility have been upon the agent being conscripted for military service (*Marshall v. Glanvill* (1917); *Morgan v. Manser* (1948)), or where as a result of war being declared one of the parties becomes an enemy alien (*Boston Deep Sea Fishing and Ice Ltd v. Farnham* (1957)) or upon the goods which the agent was to sell being expropriated (*Oxford Realty v. Annette* (1961)). A contemporary event which would frustrate the contract would be where the purpose of the agency is to trade in certain cuts of meat which are currently banned by the Government (*e.g.* T-bone steaks).

Death of either principal or agent

The death of the agent will obviously bring the relationship to an end because the relationship is a personal one which cannot (at least in theory) be delegated. The existence and particular identity of the agent lie at the very heart of the relationship. *Friend v. Young* (1897) is authority for the death of one of two agents in a joint agency terminating the authority of the survivor.

The death of the principal will usually bring the relationship to an end. This would seem to depend on whether the agent was aware of the principal's death. The normal rule is that death is a public fact of which no notice need be given. However, in *Campbell v. Anderson* (1829) the agent was factor of an estate. The principal died abroad. Being unaware of this the agent had drawn a bill of exchange in his capacity as agent. Normally in the circumstances the agent would have been personally liable on the bill but the House of Lords said that he was not in the circumstances. It would appear from Campbell that contracts entered into in good faith by an agent who is unaware of his principal's death will bind his estate. The correctness and applicability of the decision has been doubted (see Marshall, *Mercantile Law* at p. 70).

If there is more than one principal the death of any one of them has been held to bring the relationship to an end. In *Life Association of Scotland v. Douglas* (1886) a bond and disposition in security had been granted to the pursuers by a registered company and by its directors. The deed was signed by the various directors on different dates between May 11 and July 23. One of the directors died on July 4 (having signed the deed on May 11). The deed was delivered to the pursuers on July 24. The money advanced by the pursuers was not fully repaid and the life association attempted to recover from the signatories, including Douglas's executor. It was held that the implied authority given by Douglas for the delivery of the deed to the pursuers ended upon his death. The agent should be allowed to complete any transaction in which he was engaged at the time of the principal's death.

BANKRUPTCY OF THE PRINCIPAL

The bankruptcy of the principal will have the same effect on the relationship as his death. In *McKenzie v. Campbell* (1894) Fraser, a corn-factor, had been imprisoned awaiting trial. He retained Campbell, a lawyer, to act for him. He advanced Campbell money for his defence. Shortly after, on October 25, Fraser was sequestrated. McKenzie, his trustee, asked Campbell to account for the money. On December 27 Fraser was convicted. Campbell claimed that he had used up all the money advanced to him in Fraser's defence or otherwise at Fraser's instructions. It was held that the agency relationship had terminated when Fraser was sequestrated and that Campbell had to account to the trustee for all money spent after October 25. As with death, bankruptcy is a public fact of which no notice need be given. The agent may complete any transaction in which he is engaged.

BANKRUPTCY OF THE AGENT

The bankruptcy of the agent need not terminate the relationship. Whether it will, depends on whether there is an express or implied provision in the agency contract to that effect. In *McCall v. Australian Meat Co. Ltd* (1870) the bankruptcy of the agent did not terminate the relationship whereas in *Hudson v. Grainger* (1821) the bankruptcy of the agent did terminate upon the agent's bankruptcy—the court held that it was an implied provision. Arguably, given that it is the principal's capacity that is important, the agent's lack of capacity through bankruptcy is not important.

INSANITY OF EITHER PRINCIPAL OR AGENT

The insanity of the principal is generally deemed to terminate the relationship. Much will depend, however, on whether the insanity is permanent or temporary. An example of the latter can be seen in *Wink v. Mortimer* (1849). The principal had been temporarily confined to a lunatic asylum. The agent continued to act for the principal during this period and was later held to be entitled to payment for work done during the period of the principal's confinement.

A full discussion on whether insanity terminates the agency relationship can be found in *Pollok v. Paterson* (1811) (a case which was concerned with a different issue). The view taken there by the judges was that insanity of a principal was not enough on its own to terminate the relationship. Actual notice or knowledge of the insanity to or by the third party was required and thus a third party acting in good faith without knowledge of the principal's insanity is entitled to regard the agent as still having authority. In any event, the agent is allowed to complete any transactions in which he is engaged until he learns of the insanity. In England it has been held that the principal's insanity terminated the relationship, even although the agent (a solicitor) was unaware of the fact.

The Law Reform (Miscellaneous Provisions) (Scotland) Act 1990, s. 71, now provides that a factory and commission or power of attorney, granted after January 1, 1991, will continue on the subsequent mental incapacity of the granter.

THE PRINCIPAL'S BUSINESS COMING TO AN END

We saw earlier the effect of termination of fixed-term agencies. The situation is similar where the term of the agency is not stated. In *London, Leith, Edinburgh and Glasgow Shipping Co. v. Ferguson* (1850), Ferguson had been appointed as the defenders' Greenock agent. He held this post for some 20 years until the defenders intimated to him that they were no longer trading from Greenock. He claimed a year's commission on the basis that by custom of trade he was employed on a yearly basis and that that had been the terms of his employment. The court held that his position was not analogous to that of an employee (who would at that time have been hired on a yearly basis) that the defenders were entitled to end their business whenever they wished, and that there was no need to give him notice or compensation.

TERMINATION AND THIRD PARTIES

Once the relationship has been terminated, it is in the principal's best interests to inform all those who have dealt with the agent that the agent no longer has the principal's authority. If the principal fails to do so then any contracts entered into by third parties who believed in good faith that the agent was still acting with the principal's authority will bind the principal under the principle of ostensible authority. The simplest way to do this would be to contact all current customers and advertise the fact of the termination. It might be advisable to follow the statutory provisions that apply to retiring partners and are found in s. 36(1) and (2) of the Partnership Act 1890. This requires that existing customers must be contacted individually. For others, an advert in the *Edinburgh Gazette* will be sufficient notice.

8. COMMERCIAL AGENTS

Although most of the law of agency in both Scotland and England is derived from common law sources recent attempts to co-ordinate the laws of the Member States of the European Union will have an impact on some agents. Council Directive 80/653/EEC deals with certain rights and duties of "self-employed commercial agents". The Directive was implemented in the United Kingdom (although it does not apply to Northern Ireland) by means of the Commercial Agents (Council Directive) Regulations 1993 (S.I. 1993 No. 3053) and the Commercial Agents (Council Directive)(Amendment) Regulations 1993 (S.I. 1993 No. 3173). These came into force on January 1, 1994 and have retrospective effect. The Regulations are additional to the common law provisions but it should be noted that they do not apply to all agents, only those who fall within the definition of "commercial agents". There is no qualifying period before an agent comes within the provisions of the Regulations. The Regulations are, well, regulations, and only a brief discussion of the main definitions and issues is included here. There have to date been very few cases arising from the implementation of the Directive but this is bound to change. The decided cases have generally revolved around the agent's right to indemnity or compensation on termination of the agency and the issues raised are succinctly addressed by Aidan O'Neill in 1997 S.L.T. (News) 141. It may be some time, however, before the meaning and effect of the Regulations become clear. In *Page v. Combined Shipping and Trading Co. Ltd* (1997) which revolved around the agent's right to compensation, Staughton L.J. made the comment that "when this comes to trial we shall have to refer the problem to the European Court, and it will take another two years after that before a decision emerges as to what the regulation really means".

THE DEFINITION OF A COMMERCIAL AGENT

This is contained in regulation 2(1):
> "A self employed intermediary who has continuing authority to negotiate the sale or purchase of goods on behalf of another person (the 'principal'), or to negotiate and conclude the sale or purchase of goods on behalf of and in the name of that principal."

The first point to note is that the definition of a commercial agent excludes some people who we have seen are very clearly regarded as agents under common law and domestic legislation. The definition is indeed both wider and narrower than a definition under Scots law would cover. The Regulations only apply to those who are "self employed". This therefore excludes many agents who are also employees of their principal, such as sales assistants, hotel managers, etc. Also expressly excluded are:

(1) officers of a company or association (reg. 2(1)(i));
(2) partners acting on behalf of a partnership (reg. 2(1)(ii));
(3) insolvency practitioners (reg. 2);

(4) commercial agents who act gratuitously (reg. 2(2));
(5) commercial agents operating in the commodity market (reg. 2(2));
(6) Crown agents for overseas governments and administrators;
(7) agents whose activities are to be considered "secondary" (reg. 2(4)) (see below);
(8) mail order catalogue agencies for consumer goods (Sched., para. 5);
(9) consumer credit agents (Sched., para. 5).

Primary or Secondary
The Regulations only apply to commercial agents where the commercial agency is their primary activity. The Schedule to the Regulations gives some guidance as to when activities are primary and therefore covered by the Regulations. The following are covered:

(1) the commercial agent is involved on behalf of the principal in the sale or purchase of goods of a particular kind, and
(2) these sales or purchases must generally be negotiated and concluded on a commercial basis, and
(3) are likely to lead to further transaction with the customer or transactions with other customers who are either in the same geographic area or among the same group of customers, and
(4) it will be in the commercial interests of the principal in developing the market to appoint an agent who will be prepared to devote his own skill, effort and money to that end.

Paragraph 3 of the Schedule gives further indication of whether the relationship is a commercial agency. The criteria include:

(1) the principal is the manufacturer, importer or distributor of the goods, or
(2) the goods are specifically identified with the principal in the market in question, or
(3) the arrangement is described as being a commercial agency, or
(4) the agent devotes most of his time to the principal's business, or
(5) where the goods are normally only available through the principal.

Paragraph 4 of the Schedule gives indication as to when the relationship is not a commercial agency:

(1) where promotional material is supplied direct to potential customers; or
(2) if agencies are granted without reference to existing agencies in an area or within a group; or
(3) customers select goods for themselves, merely using the agent to place the order.

The only Scottish case concerning commercial agents is *King v. Tunnock Ltd* (1996). The pursuer had for many years operated a business supplying bakery products at wholesale prices to retailers. He dealt exclusively in Tunnock's products. He was not an employee. He had rented a van from them but recently it had been supplied at no charge. He paid for the petrol. Tunnock serviced and garaged the van. He wore Tunnock's overalls. He collected the bakery goods each morning from Tunnock's premises for delivery. Tunnock fixed the price at which the goods were to be sold; and a record of sales made was kept for Tunnock in a receipt book supplied by them. King was paid either in cash or by receipts made out to Tunnock or by credit account in Tunnock's name. King was paid commission on goods sold. Upon termination of the contract there was an issue as to whether King was covered by the Regulations and entitled to indemnity or compensation under regulation 17. The court held that the facts clearly pointed to the conclusion that King was a commercial agent within the definition laid down in regulation 2(1). (See also below at 60 for a discussion of King's entitlement to indemnity or compensation.)

Some issues on the definition
The Regulations are complex and, as we shall see, introduce concepts which are alien to the common law but which may in time lead to the development of the common law as more notice is taken both of the Regulations and of cases arising out of them. It is likely, however, that as the Regulations only apply to a narrowly defined group their impact may, at least in the near future, be minimal.

"Continuing authority"
The authority must be "continuing". This means that an agent who is appointed to deal with a particular transaction (or maybe a particular series of transactions) will not be covered by the Regulations.

"Authority to negotiate ... or to negotiate and conclude"
There are two alternatives here. From the wording of the regulation it would seem that all that is required to be a commercial agent is that one possesses continuing authority to negotiate. This negotiation can be exercised on behalf of the principal. This must, one imagines, cover the situation where the principal is undisclosed (see 42).

The second alternative covers the situation where the commercial agent has the continuing authority to negotiate and conclude. In this second situation, however, the power must be exercised "on behalf of *and in the name of* the principal" (emphasis added). This would obviously exclude the possibility of an undisclosed principal. The number of occasions where the agent is limited to negotiating is likely to be small, given the rationale behind the use of agents in the first place.

COMMERCIAL AGENT'S DUTIES

These are contained in regulation 3. Neither principal nor agent may derogate from their duties (reg. 5 (ii)).

The commercial agent's basic duty is to "*look after the interests of his principal and act dutifully and in good faith*" (reg. 3(1)). This means that the commercial agent must:

(1) make proper efforts to negotiate and conclude the transactions;
(2) communicate all necessary information available to the agent to the principal;
(3) comply with the principal's reasonable instructions (reg. 3(2)).

There is little here that is different from the common law duties that we looked at in Chapter 3 but there are several points that might be made.

(1) What does "to look after" the principal's interests mean? Is this the same as the common law duty to avoid a conflict of interests when buying or selling (see above at 26 *et seq*) or does it go further and mean that the agent actively has to seek out new markets, technologies, opportunities, etc., for the principal? Such an obligation would not be implied at common law. Clearly an agent who fails to avoid a conflict of interest situation will not be "looking after" the principal's interests, but that would already be covered by the common law duty.

(2) As far as "acting dutifully" is concerned this would seem to take us no further than the common law obligation to obey instructions. With regard to acting "in good faith" the idea of good faith as a general duty is one which is unfamiliar to us in the United Kingdom but familiar to Continental jurists. The Unfair Contract Terms Directive 93/13/EEC which was implemented in the United Kingdom by the Unfair Terms in Consumer Contracts Regulations 1994 (S.I. 1994 No. 3159) does, however, imply a general good faith obligation into consumer contracts. It may be that the courts will extend this duty of good faith beyond the existing fiduciary duties that have traditionally been developed in the common law but we shall have to wait and see.

Make proper efforts to negotiate and conclude the transactions he is instructed to take care of

This goes further than the common law duty to obey instructions (which is also contained in reg. 3(2) and (3)). It would seem, therefore, that an agent who fails to complete transactions because of lack of effort, laziness or general incompetence will be in breach of duty, with termination of agency by the principal being a strong possibility. This goes beyond the rules of common law.

Communicate all the necessary information available to him to the principal

This would seem to go beyond the common law duty not to misuse information. There is no common law duty to communicate information to the principal but as we saw in *Yasuda* (above at 48) the information must be available to the principal. What is or is not "necessary" will depend on the circumstances of the case. Examples, Stone suggests, would include the movement (or likely movement) of the market price of goods, activities of competitors, new products, new legislation, markets, etc.

Comply with all reasonable instructions

At common law an agent is under an obligation to obey his principal's instructions. All the regulations add is "reasonable" and that would be implied at common law (as can be seen in a whole series of employment cases).

PRINCIPAL'S OBLIGATIONS

There is a non-derogable duty imposed on the principal to act dutifully and in good faith towards his commercial agents. Some aspects of this duty of good faith are that the principal must:

(1) provide the commercial agent with the necessary documentation relating to the goods concerned (reg. 4(2)(a)).
   What this will involve will depend on the type of transaction the agent is involved in. Examples would be documents of title, import/export licences and customs documents;

(2) obtain for the agent the information necessary for the performance of the contract. Particular reference is made to the need to notify the agent within a reasonable time if the volume of transactions will be a lot less than the agent would normally have expected (reg. 4(2)(b)).
   This might include general information which would be helpful to the agent: likely customers, competitors, etc. The provision about volume of transactions will obviously help the agent manage his time to best advantage.

(3) notify the agent within a reasonable period of the principal's acceptance or refusal in relation to any transaction arranged by the agent (reg. 4(3)).

The Regulations talk about the principal's "refusal of and of any non-execution by him of a commercial transaction which the agent has procured for him". There is obviously a distinction between refusal and non-execution but what exactly it is may be grounds for debate. It may be that a refusal of a commercial transaction would involve the principal's belief that the transaction was outwith the agent's authority while non-execution would suggest something more principal centred.

AGENT'S REMUNERATION

We have already seen the approach of the common law to the agent's right to remuneration (see above at 16). The agent's rights to remuneration are contained in regulations 6 to 12. If there is no agreement as to remuneration between principal and agent then the agent is entitled to the customary and usual remuneration. If there is no such custom he is entitled to reasonable remuneration.

Most commercial agents are paid by commission and this is covered in regulations 7 to 12. Entitlement to commission will arise where "a transaction has been concluded as a result of his action". Whether or not this has been the case will presumably be decided by using the rules developed on remuneration by the common law. The Regulations, however, also provide an entitlement to commission where a transaction has been concluded with a third party whom he has previously acquired as a customer for transactions of the same kind. An agent, therefore, would still be entitled to commission if after an initial introduction the principal chooses to deal directly with the third party (perhaps to avoid paying commission).

Specific territory or group of customers

The agent is entitled during the currency of the agency agreement to commission on all transactions of the relevant type which are entered into by the principal with customers within the specific territory or group of customers. This is further protection for the agent and should prevent the principal trying to cut him out of the loop and thereby avoid paying commission. This will be the case even where the principal has concluded transactions with customers in the specific territory, without any action or effort on the agent's part (Case C–104/95 *Kontogeorgas v. Kartonpak AE* (1997)).

Post-agency transactions

The Regulations also cover situations where a transaction which has begun during the currency of the agency agreement is not in fact concluded until after the termination of the agency. The agent will be entitled to commission on such transactions provided that they were entered into within a reasonable period after the transaction terminated and that the transaction was mainly attributable to the agent's efforts during the period covered by the agency contract. This raises two questions (for which lawyers will thank the Regulations):

(1) what is a reasonable period?; and
(2) how will it be established that the transaction was "mainly attributable" to the agent's efforts?

Multi-agent claims

The Regulations also cover situations where there is a claim by more than one agent. This is designed to cover situations where there has been a change in agents, and a transaction begun under the first agent is concluded by his successor. Who is entitled to the commission? The first agent may be entitled to the commission because the contract was "mainly attributable to his [the first agent's] efforts".

There may, however, be a dispute as to whether the transaction was mainly attributable to the efforts of the first agent or his successor. The Regulations specifically allow for apportionment of commission provided the parties can agree on how this is to be done.

When is commission due?

The right to payment of commission will occur when:

(1) the principal has executed the transaction; or
(2) the principal should, according to his transaction with the third party, have executed the transaction;
(3) the third party has executed the transaction (reg. 10(1)).

The latest date on which payment of commission becomes due is when the third party has executed the agreement or when this should have occurred had the principal executed his part of the transaction. Commission must be paid not later than the last day of the month following the quarter in which it becomes due. Any attempt to derogate from these provisions to the detriment of the agent is void.

Loss of commission

There are very limited circumstances where the right to commission is lost. The only event that will occasion the agent to lose his right to commission will be where there is non-execution of the contract between principal and third party. This non-execution must be for a reason "for which the principal is not to blame". If this is the case, the right to commission will be extinguished. Examples of circumstances which would apply here are frustration or the third party not going ahead with the contract.

Supply of information

The principal is required to supply the agent with a quarterly statement of commission. This should contain an explanation of how the commission has been calculated. In addition, the agent is entitled to demand from the principal such information as will allow him to check that the commission statement is correct. This may include an extract from the "principal's books". The agent is, however, not allowed access; it is merely a requirement that the principal extract the relevant information and forward it to the agent.

TERMINATION OF AGENCY

The rules that apply to the conclusion and termination of commercial agency are to be found in Part IV of the Regulations. These provisions either supersede the provisions of the common law, or are additional or complementary to them.

At common law an agency for a fixed term will terminate at the end of the term, unless there is agreement to continue it.

In Scotland and England, unlike some European countries, there is no common law right to either indemnity or compensation upon the termination of an agency unless specifically provided for in the contract. Under the Regulations a fixed-term agency will be converted into an indefinite agency if both agent and principal continue as before after the end of the fixed term, e.g. principal issuing further instructions. An agency for an indefinite period may be terminated upon notice by either party. There are prescribed periods of notice for termination but these may be exceeded by agreement with the proviso that the principal's period of notice must not be shorter than the agent's. The minimum period is one month during the first year, two months during the second year, and three months from the start of the third year onwards. Unless the parties agree otherwise, the end of a period of notice given must coincide with the end of a calendar month.

Consequences of termination
The Regulations contain provisions whereby the agent is entitled to claim to be indemnified or compensated, in relation to losses following the termination of the agency. The provision of the right to either indemnity or compensation reflects the differing pre-regulations positions in Germany and France respectively. The agent must notify the principal within one year of the termination of the agency that he intends to make a claim. If the contract has been terminated by the death of the agent, his estate may make the claim. It is clear from the Regulations that unless there is a specific contractual provision, the agent will have to claim compensation rather than indemnity.

The agent will be entitled to an indemnity (but only if the contract so provides) where he has brought the principal new customers or has substantially increased the volume of business with existing customers and the principal continues to derive substantial business with such customers. The amount of the indemnity must be equitable having regard to all the circumstances. Particular regard will be had to lost commission in relation to the new customers. The amount of the indemnity is limited to one year's commission (based on an average over the preceding five years).

The few cases on claims for indemnity or compensation that have been decided in the United Kingdom are not particularly helpful. In *King v. Tunnock* (above), the pursuer had claimed for compensation under regulation 17(b). The sum claimed (£165,230) was calculated on the basis of his expected retirement date (10 years). The sheriff refused the compensation claim, instead awarding him three months' payment in lieu of notice. Given that the contract had been unilaterally terminated without any fault on the agent's part, Aidan O'Neill suggests in 1997 S.L.T. (News) 141 that this case was wrongly decided, but he admits that it is not clear from the sheriff's note what the basis for his decision was. In *Skingsley v. KJC Carpets Ltd* (1996) the agent sought compensation for damage due to him following the unilateral and summary termination of his agency. The contract made no provision for payment of an indemnity and the claim therefore fell to be made under the compensation provisions. The judge's eventual award of £45,000 for four years' loss of earnings was calculated by reference to the German method of calculating indemnity claims, as opposed to the French method of calculating compensation which would only have allowed for a payment of two years' gross commission (*i.e.* £22,500). Mr Skingsley was no doubt glad of the confusion in the judicial mind. The case was, however, ultimately settled out of court when the principal indicated he would appeal. This leaves us in limbo as to the correct legal reasoning in similar cases until there is clarification from the European Court of Justice.

In *Moore v. Piretta PYA Ltd* (1998) the court held that the indemnity that a commercial agent was entitled to on termination should be assessed on the basis of the value to the principal of new customers whose business the agent had been instrumental in obtaining. This amount should then be capped in accordance with the Regulations (which provide that the amount of the indemnity is limited to one year's commission). Moore had been retained under an unbroken series of contracts starting in 1988, the last of which was in 1994. He was entitled to an indemnity covering the whole of his agency. In *Moore* the value of the business brought in by the agent since the agency was terminated was £113,000. After allowable deductions the value was £92,000, which was to be reduced to £64,000 (the average commission over the preceding five years).

The agent is entitled to compensation for "damage" suffered as a result of the termination of his relationship with his principal. The Regulations list circumstances where damage will be deemed to have occurred, for example:

(1) where the termination has deprived the agent of commission which proper performance of the contract would have procured for him whilst providing his principal with substantial benefits; or

(2) in circumstances which have not enabled the commercial agent to write off the costs and expenses which he had incurred in the performance of his agency contract on the advice of his principal.

When indemnity or compensation might be lost

(1) Where the principal has terminated the agency because of the agent's conduct.

(2) Where the agent has terminated the agency unless the termination is justified:

(i) by circumstances attributable to the principal; or

(ii) on grounds of age, infirmity or illness of the agent such that he cannot reasonably be required to continue his activities; or

(iii) where the agent has, with the principal's agreement, assigned his rights and duties under the agency to another person.

Restraint of trade

The Regulations provide that a restraint of trade clause is only valid and enforceable by the principal if:

(1) it is in writing; or

(2) it only relates to the geographic area or the group of customers and the goods covered by that agent.

Any such restraint of trade clause will be valid for no more than two years after the termination of the agency.

Under common law, restraint of trade clauses are prima facie void unless they can be shown to be reasonable in the interests of the principal, the agent and the general public. Such "reasonableness" would be calculated in terms of the geographic area of the restraint, its length and the scope of business to which it is to apply. The principal would be entitled to protect a legitimate interest provided that the restriction is no wider than is needed to protect that interest. The main interest that a principal would seek to protect would be the agent's access to sensitive information. He might also wish to prevent the agent using the relationship established with third parties in the agent's own interests after (or indeed during) the agency.

There seems to be nothing in the Regulations which differs much from the common law, although the provision that a restraint of trade clause might be valid for up to two years will, on the basis of decided cases, in many instances be excessive. It is, however, a maximum.

This topic is unlikely to feature much in examinations until the jurisprudence on the Regulations develops, which may be some time. The reader should of course be aware of the main issues. The best way to do this is to study them as an add-on to the common law. The main area of interest will almost certainly centre around the provisions for indemnity, compensation and remuneration in general. Money and financial issues, generally, are a great spur to legal action and thus the development or clarification of the law.

APPENDIX: SAMPLE EXAMINATION QUESTIONS AND ANSWER PLANS

EXAMINATION TECHNIQUE

The questions that follow are similar to those that are asked in most examinations where agency is part of the syllabus. The suggested answers are not the only answers to the questions. Most problem questions in law exams have more than one correct answer. More important than your conclusion is the justification for your conclusion. In exams both knowledge and technique are important: You should aim to develop both. There is not enough room here to advise you on the best method to acquire, retain and understand the substantive legal knowledge you need to pass the exam but it may be useful to make some brief points on technique.

IN GENERAL

- Read all the questions in the paper before you start writing. This may seem like a waste of time but it pays dividends. As you decide which questions you are going to answer, jot down the main issues, cases and statutes that are relevant.
- An exam is not the wedding feast at Cana. Do not keep your best questions until the end. Do them first. You will be fresher, which is important, but more importantly so will the examiner.
- Try to divide your time as equally as possible, although there is no point spending time on a question about which you know little or nothing. If you run out of time on a particular question, answer it in note form. The examiner can only give you credit for what is on the page. A page of notes that cover most of the issues raised will be better than two or three beautifully crafted sentences that do no more than introduce the topic.

- The examiner is not your enemy. Short of bribery, you should keep him as sweet as possible. Ways of doing so include writing legibly. Avoid the urge to write in multi-coloured ink. Underlining cases and statutes also helps. Avoid jokes and irrelevant material: both will cost you time and it is best to let the examiner believe he is the comedian.

IN SPECIFIC

- Identify the issues raised by the question. There is unlikely to be only one. Do this at the start of your answer.
- Approach the issues in turn. Explain the law that is relevant to the legal issues raised by the question. Back up what you say by reference to either statute (which in agency will be rare) or case law. Most examiners are so lacking in imagination that the facts in problem questions are usually a mere retelling of a decided case. Do not panic if you cannot remember the name of the case. "A case about" will be acceptable. It is your understanding of the law that is being tested.
- In conclusion link the discussion of the law to the facts of the case. Remember to do what the question asks you to do. Do not advise Peter if the question asks you to advise Paul. This mistake may not be fatal but is best (and easily) avoided.
- Try to manage your exam so that you have time to re-read your answers. This is as important as the time spent reading all the questions at the start.

QUESTION 1

For many years Bilbo owned and ran a highly successful pub, "The Gandalf Arms". Following an expensive and acrimonious divorce he has had to sell the pub to Orc Brewers plc. Aware of how much his personal input contributed to the pub's profits, Orc have retained Bilbo as manager and he is still the licensee. Indeed nothing seems to have changed. The brewery have, however, told Bilbo that in future he must order all beer through them, and spirits and soft drinks, etc., must be ordered through one of Orc's "preferred wholesalers". The new beer is not popular with a vocal minority of "old hands", so Bilbo has ordered a consignment of beer from one of his old suppliers. This seems to have done the trick. Bilbo has also been offered an exceptionally good price on "alcopops", from a company which is not on the "preferred" list. He knows he can sell these at a good price to his teenage customers. The sales representative, who is a customer of Bilbo, tells him that in return for his order the company will supply all the alcohol for Bilbo's sudden and forthcoming wedding. Bilbo signs the order.

Bilbo had thought of converting some unused rooms in the pub into an Internet café. He has not consulted Orc about this but has approached a local builder and a local computer firm. At a site meeting, as they know he no longer owns the pub, they ask him if the plans have been approved by

Orc. Bilbo assures them it was all their managing director's idea in the first place. Just then, one of Orc's directors arrives on the scene. Bilbo introduces him to the others but no more than social pleasantries are exchanged. The work has been carried out and the café is up and running. The old hands and the teenagers are all happy. Orc's managing director arrives, discovers the whole tale, is not at all pleased, and has indicated that he will not authorise payment of any of the bills—and his plans for Bilbo are unprintable.

Discuss the issues raised.

Suggested answer

Outline

Agent's authority/Agent's representations/Agent's liability
Agent's duty of good faith: consequences of breach of good faith

One of the core issues in agency is that of authority. Without authority there is generally no agency. There are, of course, exceptions to this such as necessity and the possibility of ratification of unauthorised acts. Generally speaking, the principal will be bound by acts of an agent who is acting *THEN* within his authority. When Bilbo was the owner of the pub the question of *NOW* authority (and, indeed, agency) was not an issue. It is now, however. As manager of the pub Bilbo has the authority to act within the limits set by the brewery; as we have seen they have placed some specific restrictions on this authority. However, in addition to the authority which the brewery have given him, the agent also has implied authority to do anything which is necessary and incidental to the job he does. In addition, the agent may have ostensible or apparent authority. This is authority which has been neither expressly nor impliedly conferred on the agent but is authority which the agent has because of the conduct of principal and agent and also because of a representation by the principal that the agent is acting on his behalf. The representation should, it must be noted, come from the principal. It should also be remembered that personal bar by holding out may operate. The principal may have withdrawn the agent's authority but failed to notify third parties. On the other hand, the third party may know of the limitations, or be deemed to know them from the status of the agent.

When Bilbo contracted for the beer and the alcopops, he was acting outwith his actual authority. The brewery, however, are likely to be liable under the contract on the ground that, as placed, this order was within the implied authority of the manager of a pub. This was the decision in *Watteau v. Fenwick* where the court held that the principal was liable for all acts which were within the authority usually conferred on an agent of that category. Ordering beer and spirits would normally be within a pub manager's authority; therefore the brewery may well be liable. However, in *Daw v. Simmins,* where the facts are similar to those of *Watteau* and Bilbo, the court reached a different decision. The difference in *Daw* was that the third party was aware of the fact that the pub was owned by a brewery and that there would therefore be restrictions placed on the manager's authority. Much would depend, therefore, on the knowledge of the respective third parties.

Bilbo owes Orc a duty to act in good faith. One aspect of this duty is the duty to accept no secret commissions or bribes. Bilbo, when entering into the contract for the alcopops, has accepted a "gift" of alcohol for his wedding. Whether this is a secret commission or a bribe in the criminal sense is to a certain extent immaterial. A bribe is any inducement which is kept secret from the principal (*Anangel Atlas Compania Naviera*). Whether it is a bribe or secret commission, the cost of the alcohol must be paid over to Orc, who may choose to dismiss Bilbo and rescind the contract for the alcopops, etc. There may be (although unlikely here) criminal consequences but these are outwith the hands of the parties.

In addition, Bilbo may incur personal liability for the "alcopops" because he has signed the order personally. Much will depend on whether it was clear when he signed that he was merely signing as an agent. In *Stone & Rolfe v. Kimber Coal* the addition of the word "for" was enough to relieve the agent of liability. If Bilbo signed in his own name then he might be personally liable, as in *Stewart v. Shannessy* where there was no indication from the signature that it was being signed as an agent only.

With regard to the contract for the Internet café Bilbo has clearly acted outwith his authority. It is unlikely that commissioning work of this kind would come under either the implied or the ostensible authority of a pub manager and if this is the case then the brewery would not be liable. The visit of the director to the pub might prevent the brewers from denying authority, but on the facts this seems unlikely. In any event, in *Armagas v. Mundogas* the court held that where there is nothing beyond the agent's own false assertion that he has authority, the principal will not be bound. The issue here would be, did the third parties know that Bilbo would not generally have the authority to enter this type of contract? Bilbo, when questioned, expressly stated that he had the authority. On similar facts in *Armagas*, the Lords held that the principal was not bound. More favourable to the third parties is the decision in *First Energy (U.K.) Ltd* where the third party knew that the agent lacked the authority to enter into a particular contract, as he knew the decisions were made in the bank's head office. The court held that the agent had apparent authority to communicate head office decisions. The principal was bound by the transaction entered into by the agent because it was reasonable for him to believe that the principal had given him the authority. The question will be whether it was reasonable for the third parties to rely on Bilbo's statement that he had been authorised by the MD to enter into the contract. It is unlikely that a claim of personal bar based on the director's visit to the pub would be successful.

If Orc are not liable on the contracts for the beer, the alcopops and the café then Bilbo may himself be liable for breach of warranty of authority (*Anderson v. Croall*).

QUESTION 2

Skinner is your client; he runs an estate agency. He has come to see you in a state of some distress. He seems to have upset some of his clients over his behaviour in some recent transactions. He wants you to sort it all out for him.

(1) Skinner had been retained to sell some old commercial property in the canal area of the city on behalf of Peter, an elderly businessman and client. The area where the property is situated is generally run down and Peter is unsure what the property will fetch. A surveyor friend of Peter has suggested it might fetch £200,000. Skinner is aware that a London development company, of which his brother is managing director, is interested in converting canal-side commercial property into loft apartments. He has arranged the sale of the property to the development company for £150,000 on the understanding that when the property is converted he and his three children will each be given one of the lofts. Peter has heard rumours about all this and is none too happy; he is saying he will not now go ahead with the sale.

(2) Skinner has also been retained under a "sole agency" agreement to sell Sarah's house. The sale agency is to last six months. During that time plenty of people view the flat but nobody buys it. However, Sarah has seen a "House Wanted" ad in the paper and has replied. The advertiser views the house, likes it and buys the house after the expiry of the sale agency agreement. Skinner feels that Sarah has "cheated him" out of his rightful commission and wants to know where he stands.

(3) Skinner has also been retained to sell Carol's house (semi-detached). It has been on sale for a couple of weeks and there are no takers. Her next-door neighbour approaches Skinner and asks him to sell his house. It sells immediately and the purchaser, on discovering that Carol's house is also for sale, says he will buy it as well. For no reason that makes sense to Skinner, Carol is extremely unhappy; she says he was her agent and should not have acted for her neighbour or, if he did, he should have asked her. He feels he has acted correctly.

Discuss the issues raised.

Suggested answer

Outline

Agency/Agent's rights/Agent's duties
Fiduciary nature of agency/Multi-principal situations/Secret commissions

(1) Although estate agents do not fulfil exactly the same role as most other agents, the common law rules on agency are deemed to apply to them and, additionally, there is statutory regulation of those running an estate agency under the Estate Agents Act 1979 and the Property Misdescriptions Act 1991. The issues raised by the question, however, relate to the common law rights and duties of principal and agent. These rights and duties may be specifically addressed in the contract between the parties or, in the absence of such provision, they may be implied into the contract by common law. The issues raised in the question revolve around the agent's duty to act in good faith and in the best interests of his

principal, and the agent's rights to be remunerated by the principal for the performance of his agency.

The relationship of principal and agent is one which is generally seen as falling into a special category as it involves a special degree of trust, being as it is a fiduciary relationship. The principal has to trust the agent to act in the principal's best interests and the agent has to trust the principal to pay him and relieve him of liabilities. The nature and extent of this fiduciary duty may not be as all-encompassing as it was previously thought to be. In *Lothian v. Jenolite* (1969) the court held that there was no universally implied prohibition that an agent would never compete with his principal. Obviously the situation would be different where the agent had agreed never to compete. Further, in *Sao Paulo Alpargatas S.A. v. Standard Chartered Bank Ltd* (1985) the court held that the agent need act in his principal's interests only while acting in the course of his agency. Both of these cases may be relevant to Skinner's dispute with Sarah.

The issues raised by Skinner's transactions on behalf of Peter involve a breach of the agent's duty to act in good faith for the benefit of his principal. The agent should not allow his own personal interests to come into conflict with those of his principal. If there is the likelihood of any such conflict the agent should inform the principal of the circumstances. The agent's duty of good faith has several aspects to it. The first aspect that concerns us here is that the agent is under a duty not to use his position as an agent to make any profit from the agency over and above the remuneration he receives from the principal. What we are dealing with here are what are known as secret profits or secret commissions or in some cases bribes. An example of a secret profit can be seen in *Ronaldson v. Drummond & Reid* (1881) where a solicitor, who was entrusted to send goods to auction, arranged with the auctioneer that he would receive half the sales commission. He had to account for the payment. Other examples of secret commissions might include discounts received by the agent (*Turnbull v. Gorden* (1869)). It does not matter that the principal could not have obtained the discount himself, as in *SEAL v. McIver*, and has been held to extend to windfall gains as in *Trans Barwil Agencies v. John S. Braid* (1988) where, due to incorrect exchange rates being used, the agent received more than he should have. It had to be paid over to the principal. More than the above seems to be at issue here. Skinner would definitely seem to have a conflict of interest, given his brother's position in the property company. The arrangement over the provision of the lofts to Skinner and his family looks very much like a bribe. A bribe was defined in *Industries and General Mortgage Co. v. Lewis* (1949) as a payment made to an agent by a third party who knows the agent is an agent, and which the agent fails to disclose to the principal.

In *Anangel Compania Naviera SA (1990) v. Ishikawajima-Harima Heavy Industries Ltd* (1990) the court held that the key element in whether a payment was a bribe or a secret commission was whether the payment gave rise to a conflict of interest. It can be argued that Skinner already has a conflict because of his brother's involvement and the provision of the lofts here exacerbates it. The below-valuation sale would seem to confirm this.

If Peter feels that there was bribery involved he may wish to involve the police. His own interests, however, would be better served by raising civil proceedings against both Skinner and the property company. He can recover any commission paid to Skinner, refuse to pay any due (but see *United Turkey Red* which will allow such refusal only for the period when Skinner was in breach). As far as the property company is concerned, Peter can refuse to go ahead with the sale and seek to recover the value of the secret commission.

(2) Skinner's problems with Sarah concern the agent's right to be remunerated by the principal. If there is no express provision as to remuneration, the agent will generally be entitled to be paid professional rates, or a reasonable amount. Disputes frequently arise between estate agents and their clients as to the former's entitlement to commission on a sale. The approach taken by the courts will generally be to discover if the sale was the result of the agent's efforts. If this is so, then the agent will be entitled to be paid. In *Walker, Fraser & Steele v. Fraser's Trustees* (1910) the court held that the entitlement to commission was dependent on the agent contributing in a major way to the sale. This was also the view in *Chris Hart v. Currie* (1992). In *Harwood v. Smith* (1997) the facts are very similar to those in the question. In *Harwood* the court felt that the agent would be due commission after the six months if he had either introduced the purchaser or negotiated with the purchaser on the seller's behalf. Neither of these applied in *Harwood*, nor do they in Sarah's case. No commission is therefore due.

(3) The facts in Carol's case are similar to those in *Kelly v. Cooper* (1992). The issue in *Kelly* was whether by acting for more than one principal the agent was in breach of his duty to act in good faith. It was clear from *Lothian v. Jenolite* (1969) that there was no implied condition that the agent will never act in a way that may conflict with his principal's interests. In *Kelly* the agent was held not to have breached his duty of good faith, nor had there been a conflict of interest. It is clear from *Kelly* that there is a conflict of interest in Carol's situation. The conflict is, however, between the two principals: Carol and her neighbour. It was clear from *Kelly* that an estate agent need not disclose all relevant information to one principal, if this will result in a breach of duty to another.

QUESTION 3

On the first day of your traineeship the senior partner has asked you to prepare briefing notes on the following:

(1) One of the firm's clients, Tom, was a director of a plc. He was also one of the company's promoters. The company has had a brief but eventful life and has gone into (members' voluntary) liquidation. This has caused quite a few people to lose money and, following a police investigation, Tom has now been arrested and charged with fraud on the ground that he had misapplied company funds and issued a fraudulent prospectus.

He knows he will not qualify for legal aid and wants to know if the company will be liable to pay for the costs of his defence.

(2) Another client, Brian, has approached the firm for advice. He is known to be a bit of a "car nut" but has no formal training as a mechanic. One of his colleagues, Sally, who was wanting to buy a car but knew nothing about cars, asked Brian to buy a car on her behalf. Brian said he would be happy to do so, and would not accept any payment. Sally was insistent that she did not want a car that had been involved in an accident. Brian spotted a likely car, noticed that there had been some repainting done and the car had a new bonnet but made no inquiries. He bought it, but it has subsequently proven to be unsatisfactory and, more importantly, has been discovered to have been written off by an insurance company following a head-on collision. Sally is understandably upset and Brian wants to know where he stands.

(3) A local clothes shop signed an "exclusive" deal with "Assylum" a fashionable clothing manufacturer, under which they would sell only that manufacturer's clothes. They were happy to do so for several years, but the label is no longer as fashionable and the shop has started to sell other manufacturers' clothes as well. Assylum has discovered this and has informed the shop that it is terminating the agreement and is also refusing to pay sales commission due to the shop on goods sold on behalf of Assylum.

Prepare briefing notes.

Suggested answer

Outline

Agency/Agency rights/Rights to be relieved of liability
Gratuitous agents/Standard of care
Agent's Remuneration/Entitlement when agent in breach

The issues raised in this question are concerned with the agent's right to be relieved of all losses, liabilities and expenses incurred in the course of the agency and the agent's right to be paid when he, the agent, has breached his obligations to the principal. The other issue is the obligation of an agent to exercise reasonable care in the performance of his agency, with particular reference to situations where the agent is acting gratuitously.

(1) Under normal circumstances the agent will incur neither rights nor obligations under the contract and in the event that he does incur such obligations the principal will normally be expected to relieve him of them. In *Dinesmann v. Mair* it would seem to have been the case that the agent could deduct the expense of such obligations from money he was holding on the principal's behalf. Another example can be seen in *Drummond v. Cairns* where the agent was instructed to buy shares for the principal, which the principal failed to pay for when due. The agent had to sell the shares at

a loss; his loss had to be made good by the principal. There will, however, be circumstances where the principal will not have to make good the agent's losses. An example would be where the agent has acted carelessly or negligently, as in *Davison v. Fernandes* where the principal was induced to sell shares on the basis of wrong information given by the agent. Another circumstance which will mean the principal need not relieve the agent of liability is where the agent has acted illegally. In *Tomlinson v. Liquidators of Scottish Amalgamated Silks* the facts are similar to those involving Tom. On the basis of *Tomlinson* it would be unlikely that Tom will have the costs of his defence met by the company.

(2) All agents are under an obligation to exercise reasonable skill and care. The standard of skill and care will depend on the circumstances. A higher standard will be expected of qualified tradesmen and professionals than will be expected of a friend. An agent who fails to exercise reasonable care may be liable in damages to the principal. The obligation to act with reasonable care extends not only to agents who are paid but also to agents who act gratuitously. Such agents are known as mandatories and, according to Bell, are under an obligation to exercise reasonable care. The case of *Copland v. Brogan* is useful to understand what reasonable care means. There the mandatory lost money belonging to the mandant. There was no suggestion of dishonesty but the court held that losing money without a satisfactory explanation meant that the mandatory had failed to exercise reasonable care. Reasonable care was behaving as you would with your own property. In *Chaudry v. Prabhakar* the facts are much the same as in Sally's case. The court held that, while it chose not to say exactly what standard of care applied to an unpaid agent, all that is required is to consider whether in the circumstances of a particular case there has been a sufficient standard of care; it was obvious that the agent in that case had failed to meet it. It would therefore be likely that Brian would be liable in damages to Sally.

(3) The issues raised by the clothes shop's failure to keep to their agreement generally revolve around the right of the agent to be paid for his services (which in part has been addressed in Question 2). However, the failure also raises issues as to the agent's duty to obey the principal's instructions. Only instructions that are lawful and reasonable have to be obeyed. An agent who fails to obey instructions will usually be personally liable to the agent and, possibly, to third parties should loss result. This liability will be subject to the need for the principal to minimise his loss and where the agent has failed to follow the principal's instructions the principal will not have to pay him for that period. This was the case in *Graham v. United Turkey Red Co. Ltd* which is similar to the question. On the basis of *Graham* it would seem that Assylum would need to pay the shop the agreed commission but only for the period before they started selling the other manufacturers' goods.

QUESTION 4

Under what circumstances can agency be established by ratification and what is the effect of such ratification?

Suggested answer

Outline

What is ratification? Limitation on ratification
Retrospective effect of ratification

The creation of agency normally involves the principal specifically giving the agent authority to act on the principal's behalf before the agent enters any transactions. Ratification, however, arises in two situations. In the first situation a person who has no authority at all purports to act on behalf of another person. In the second situation the agent does have authority to act but he exceeds it, and enters an unauthorised contract. Although in both these situations the contract is unauthorised and therefore not binding on the principal, he may choose to ratify or indicate his approval of what the "agent" has done. Ratification has retrospective effect: it is as if the agent had had authority all along (*Bolton Partners v. Lambert*). Of course, there is no obligation on the principal to ratify the agent's actions and, if he chooses not to do so, the agent will be personally liable to the third party for breach of warranty of authority. There are, however, limits on the creation of agency by ratification.

First, the agent must have contracted as an agent and have named his principal. If the principal's existence or name has not been disclosed, the undisclosed principal cannot ratify. The leading case here is *Keighley, Maxsted & Co. v. Durant* where an agent was authorised to buy wheat at a certain price by his principal. He bought the wheat at a slightly higher price and in his own name. The undisclosed principal purported to ratify the contract but later refused to take delivery of the wheat. The seller of the wheat was unable to sue the agent, who was insolvent, and sued the principal. His attempt failed on the grounds that the existence of an agency was not known at the time of the contract, and an undisclosed principal cannot ratify. The decision in *Keighley* is inconsistent with the otherwise accepted rule that an undisclosed principal can both sue and be sued on a contract. It may well be the case that in Scotland *Keighley* would not be followed. In *Lockhart v. Moodie,* where the facts were similar to *Keighley,* the principal was held liable to the extent of the price he had authorised the agent to pay. It could also be argued that the agent's actions in *Keighley* were within his implied authority.

Secondly, the principal must have had contractual capacity both at the time the contract was made and also at the date of the purported ratification. The classic example of lack of contractual capacity was a contract entered into by the directors of a company where such contract was beyond the powers of the company. Traditionally, such a contract could not be ratified but now it can be ratified by special resolution (Companies Act 1985, s. 35(3)). Also, if the principal was an enemy alien when the contract was made, any subsequent attempted ratification would be ineffective (*Boston Deep Sea Fishing and Ice Co. v. Farnham*).

Thirdly, the principal must have been in existence both at the date of the contract and of the ratification. Anyone who purports to act for a company prior to its incorporation may fall foul of this requirement. In *Kelner v.*

Baxter it was held that the attempt by the company to ratify an earlier contract was ineffective. Any liability arising from the contract falls upon those making it. Regard should also be had to s. 36C of the Companies Act 1985 which states that a person acting as agent or for the company will be personally liable unless there is an express agreement to the contrary (*Phonogram v. Lane*).

Fourthly, the principal must ratify the act in time. This will usually be within a reasonable time. What is a reasonable time will depend on the circumstances. In *Metropolitan Asylums Boards Managers v. Kingham* it was held that a contract cannot be ratified after the contract is due to begin. This was not the view taken in *Bedford Insurance v. Instituto de Resseguros do Brazil* where it was held that ratification after the time for performance is permissible where it would be to the benefit of the third party. There may also be a requirement that the contract be ratified within a specified time, as in *Goodall v. Bilsland*. Regard should also be had to the position with insurance contracts (*Grover v. Matthews* and the Marine Insurance Act 1906).

Lastly, the principal must have full knowledge of all relevant facts (*Savery v. King*).

The effect of a principal validly ratifying a contract is to make the principal retrospectively liable on the contract from the date it was made. The agent's authority has, as it were, been backdated. This may cause difficulties for third parties (*Bolton v. Lambert*). The third party may also face problems should the principal choose not to ratify but in such an event he can sue the agent for breach of warranty of authority (*Anderson v. Croall*).

INDEX